SHOWING OFF

Philip L. Wagner

Showing Off
The Geltung Hypothesis

 University of Texas Press, Austin

First edition, 1996

Requests for permission to reproduce material from this work should be sent to Permissions, University of Texas Press, Box 7819, Austin, TX 78713-7819.

⊚ The paper used in this publication meets the minimum requirements of American National Standard for Information Sciences—Permanence of Paper for Printed Library Materials, ANSI Z39.48-1984.

LIBRARY OF CONGRESS CATALOGING-IN-PUBLICATION DATA

Wagner, Philip L. (Philip Laurence), 1921 –
    Showing off: the Geltung hypothesis / by Philip L. Wagner. — 1st ed.
       p.   cm.
    Includes bibliographical references and index.
    ISBN 0-292-79102-X (alk. paper). — ISBN 0-292-79103-8 (pbk. : alk. paper)
    1. Human geography. 2. Attention-seeking. 3. Prestige.
4. Communication. 5. Man—Influence on nature. 6. Genetic psychology. I. Title.
GF50.W34   1996
304.2—dc20   95-50184

CONTENTS

Economics, ethics, and ecology have yet to make peace. The results and the portents give just cause for concern, indeed for alarm.

The defects in our understanding and decisions that bear responsibility for this dangerous disparity of viewpoints lie deeper than the incompatibility among the methods and objectives of the disciplines concerned. They reflect a stubborn dualistic tendency that conceives of human life and action as somehow separate and altogether different from physical, material reality.

In contrast, we may however conceive of humanity and all its acts and works as nothing other than the product of, and participant in, entirely normal natural processes. The unifying perspective thus obtained allows a reinterpretation of the role of the individual in nature, and the role of nature in people themselves, that carries major implications for the ways we think and act.

The present essay represents one frankly speculative step in progress toward the goal of such a conception. It draws on diverse kinds of evidence and presents a materialist and evolutionary selectionist perspective.

For many years I have sought to develop a clearer view of the human use of the earth and the relationships between environments and peoples. Among the publications that resulted I shall cite two earlier steps on this path. The concluding paragraphs from two of my previous books embody the standpoints attained: "The very original role of man [*sic!*] in nature is consequent upon the biological peculiarities of the human species. Man is inherently a restless remaker of his own world" (Wagner 1960:237).

That conclusion called for further elaboration. The next step was suggested in the last few sentences of a subsequent book: "Geography records the expression of men transforming environments, calling entire peoples into being. The palimpsest of earth preserves the traces of untold assertions of the human will and spirit, one inscription on another, half illegible. Deciphered even tentatively (for that is all their state permits) they restore a tale of culture living, moving, growing through communication" (Wagner 1972:102).

That very tale of the way that culture lives, moves, and grows had yet to be told, and with it the tale of transformed environments. The old complacent invocation of a mystery called culture would not do. Human communication, I had become convinced, must account for how culture—and cultures—develop and operate, and hence how people think and act.

But the premise already adopted requires a biological account of communication processes. The traditional emphasis on supposed content and meanings of discourse, on semiotic aspects, cannot satisfy this condition. Instead, I began to conceive of communication as a natural form of physical activity reflecting the genetic program evolved in the human species and describable in straightforward material terms.

A mere mechanical description of human communicative activity would, nevertheless, deserve in itself little interest. It is rather the effects of that particular activity on other forms of behavior that matter infinitely more and carry profound social and ecological consequences. Communication between individuals exerts a clear selective influence upon ensuing behavior and through it on relationships among people and on their overall ecological situation. Conversely, we can postulate that the anticipated consequences of communicative acts exercise a certain selective effect upon potential utterances. This essay, in effect, concerns what may finally govern the choices resulting and proposes an underlying genetic predisposition in all human individuals toward a specific communicative strategy it describes, as well as attempting to detail some concrete implications for human social life and for habitats and environment.

The thesis this essay advances amounts to a personal world-view, developed out of intimate personal experience as well as years of travel and observation, reading wide and diverse, and much discussion. I cannot attempt to record all the articles and books that have helped shape my argument, and so I beg the reader's indulgence for omitting detailed citations to most of them. My wide-ranging conjectures piece together highly varied notions and findings from numerous seemingly unrelated sources, but I hope this mere essay sums up a consistent and cohesive viewpoint that invites unconventional thinking and may encourage further research. The argument holds implications for practical action, as well as for economics, ethics, and ecology, and for the study of human society.

I owe a permanent debt to authors far too numerous to name, especially to so many associates and colleagues that I cannot hope to mention more than a few of them. The lively, unconstrained discussions in the Pi Digamma Seminar at Simon Fraser University, as well as conversations during semesters spent in Austin and Baton Rouge, contributed to shaping the argument. I must however acknowledge my special obligation to my wife, Margret, son, Tom, and cousin Richard; to the late Alfredo Hurtado and David Sopher; in particular to Andrew Gunder Frank, Marilyn and Gary Gates, Torsten Hägerstrand, and Peter Rowbotham; and to Augustin Berque, Tommy Carlstein, Paul Claval, Douglas Deur, Paul W. English, Robert Geipel, Peter Griffiths, Gerhard Hard, Hiroshi Tanaka Shimazaki, Gerald Patchell, and Shue Tuck Wong, among many others, for their generous patience, encouragement, and criticism. Thanks also to one anonymous referee whose detailed comments helped much. Despite all such kindness and insight, the blunders and faults are my own.

● SHOWING OFF

The Geltung Hypothesis •

Recent research on brain-damaged infants has revealed an astonishing feature of the human genetic endowment. A few individuals suffering so deep an impairment of the functions of the right hemisphere that they are utterly unable to perform such elementary tasks as feeding themselves, or tying their shoelaces, nevertheless retain a striking ability not only to communicate in fluent grammatical speech but also to display their emotions and relate to other people through eloquent and appealing gestures and facial expressions (Bellugi et al., 1991, 1992). The engaging, ingratiating behavior of such individuals bespeaks more than language capacity: it reveals a more comprehensive inborn program that must underlie and facilitate the marked sociality of the human species.

This rare condition, referred to as Williams' Syndrome, unmistakably indicates that individuals of our species innately possess a propensity to influence, and especially to attract and appeal to, other people through both language and additional displays, powerfully effective in establishing and managing social bonds. We are born to be show-offs.

In this book I attempt to argue for the same conclusion, drawing on utterly different evidence. In fact, the information on Williams' Syndrome turned up just after completion of the penultimate draft of this work. The quite unexpected convergence of firm neuropsychological discoveries with my own rather eclectic conjectures on human behavior doubly declares that human beings are innately programmed to persistently and skillfully cultivate attention, acceptance, respect, esteem, and trust from their fellows—to strive for what I call Geltung.

So commonplace a notion arises readily out of our daily experience and has been advanced in literary works for centuries, but somehow it has heretofore failed to be seen as momentous for scientific understanding of humanity's life and agency on earth. Except for the revelations concerning Williams' Syndrome, the scientific evidence remains minimal, admittedly; my boldest hope is that of inviting research and fundamental reflection on some of the questions here raised.

The Geltung Hypothesis this book presents is a frank attempt to reinterpret human nature and, in particular, motivation on the basis of the foregoing notion of a specific strong social instinct. It maintains that the craving for Geltung and the action that cultivates it are central to our innate behavioral program and that personal Geltung exerts a decisive influence in social relationships and activities, and hence on what we do to the world.

This hypothesis has been conceived as a part of an even more ambitious vision, that of a dynamic and diversified humanity participating fully in natural physical processes to transform and reorganize its earthly habitats and the global environment. The implications are not merely social and psychological, but ecological too.

Human nature and motivation constitute a conspicuous blind spot in the ecological perspective. Compared to other organisms, this species appears to behave in distressingly unpredictable and often counteradaptive ways. A secure understanding of the basic ecological characteristics and capacities of human individuals and of the relevant controls in the human genetic program is urgently needed, and of course it must entail a much revised and clearer conception of those prominent universal features of humanity's behavior that are its sociality and so-called cultural propensities.

The Geltung Hypothesis spotlights the special communicative mechanisms underlying the social and cultural features of human ecology—specifically the governing function of one indispensable ecological relationship, that among the members of the species itself—in human reproductive success and survival as well as in the human agency in nature in general. That central relationship among individuals and social groups is maintained, mediated, and unceasingly modified by elaborated communication mechanisms or displays, including language and much more. The latter exist and are programmed, the hypothesis holds, above all to assure the Geltung that serves to integrate the individual into the social universe and to enable joint social enterprise and mutual increase of learning and, hence, intervention in nature.

The agency of human enterprise proclaims itself in an intricate geography of transformed environment and habitats and in impressively structured spaces. Yet geographers themselves persist in describing the world as if it consisted of two disparate realities, one physical or natural, the other cultural or human, and perhaps most of the general public, at least in the West, also sees it thus. But all the world is both truly physical and necessarily natural, while much of it too declares the human impact. The challenge of constructing a single unitary vision of our world and ourselves within it has remained to be addressed. In order to meet that challenge it cannot suffice alone to document variety among the inhabited spaces of the earth and consign their explanation to the inscrutable black box of culture.

The facts and character of culture must be accounted for themselves, and this accounting calls for comprehension of how the bearers and executors of culture behave in earthly space and time. The Geltung Hypothesis treats of this behavior. It portrays the world of human beings as consisting of occasions of encounter and exchange, in "spaces of human display," established and identified by interpersonal actions. Influence and imitation among individuals, impelled by personal Geltung, result according to this view in the wide spatial distribution of invented activity routines as well as of objects and impart a common cultural coloration to varied whole areas and populations. This imitative diffusional process is implemented by subsisting social networks and their spatial pathways and often is consolidated by constructed physical facilities. Culture, on this interpretation, at a given moment and locality amounts simply to the temporary and complex legacy of a multitude of such imitative diffusions of invented routines over time, from many disparate sources.

The Geltung-favored (and Geltung-seeking) initiative of certain individuals avails itself of the social cohesion and collaboration that it can muster, along with imitatively learned culture, in order to inspire and guide the transformation of the habitat and modify environmental relationships. This enterprise creates its own display of varied landscapes and its own ecological conditions. According to the hypothesis, such initiative and influence, exercised by individuals both courting and commanding special Geltung, result in cultural diffusion and common enterprise alike, which together determine how well human groups maintain themselves and sustain secure environmental, ecological adjustments.

As both technical powers and the communicative integration of humanity increase apace, the magnitude of ecological change grows ever vaster and along with its promise brings perils as well. It is in the end individual human beings who, however associated with their fellows, summoning the powers of technology, make this change for better or for worse, and particular people among them who, by virtue of their own Geltung and in quest for still greater Geltung, organize and manage the collective effort.

The following chapter considers the ecological role of the human individual, in particular the potentialities of the communicative use of the body.

Bodies Influence Bodies ●

We are out in the forest, somewhere in Canada. In some distant city, a construction company has set today's schedule for the dynamite crew on the site. At a word from the chief engineer, a half mile away, a worker throws a switch. The mountain erupts into cascades of pebbles and boulders crashing down the raw slope. Communication and control—and voilà, the face of nature is rearranged!

Communication consists of conveying or imparting something, some impulse, over a given distance, presumably to some receiver. It implies a connection, if not always control.

Those miniscule flows of energy expended in the engineer's or anyone else's communication can aspire to command, to some extent, the infinitely vaster energies of nature. They can only do so, to be sure, by mustering the concerted and complementary energies of human collectivities in order to implement and manage the technological processes serving (or sometimes thwarting) human ends.

Communication can transcend and conquer distance and space. It can even reach forward through time. And through communication human beings gain immense powers to transform environments. Our very act of communicating creates its own spaces and landscapes and relies on transformed environments to produce its effects. Utterly necessary for human ecological survival, it is also—and therefore—the key to social survival. Shaped under natural selection, it must also contribute to the differential perpetuation of particular genetic traits in humanity. As it operates to serve these ends, communication incorporates the individual

not only into an environment or habitat, and into a place or community, but also into a geographical universe of regions and boundaries,
places and networks, as well as societal and cultural universes of interdependence and conflict, subjection or dominance. In addition, it makes
humanity a major agent of change in the physical world.

In promoting and implementing intense sociality, human communication compensates, in a particular way, for the physical limitations of
the body. Thus it operates as a decisive ecological factor.

Conspicuous prey because of their size but woefully short of built-in
defenses; weaklings amid the great beasts; lickerish but finicky about
their food, among voracious competitors; almost unique in their natural
nakedness, compared to other land mammals, human beings would appear to be rather poor candidates for ecological dominance. What could
they do? Stick together!

Who could predict, just on the basis of human anatomy, that this
puny creature would compose symphonies, build cities, fight wars, and
travel to the moon? The gross structure and composition of the body, at
least, give no indications of such potentialities, aside perhaps from the
mysteries enshrined within the strikingly hypertrophied, heavily con-
voluted brain. According to their bodies' other gross features, one might
expect human beings at most to excel at the normal business of apes. In
fact, the individual human body, entirely alone, cannot accomplish any
more than that, if as much.

Obviously, from a physical standpoint, a human being can do only
what a body can do. Everyone does have to activate the muscles autono-
mously. Therefore only individuals can do things. Even when acting
collectively, collaborating, they have to operate their own bodies for
themselves. What we know human beings can accomplish, therefore,
seems all out of proportion to the humble body's modest inherent
capacities.

Everything that human beings actually do upon this earth, then, every
change they accomplish in their surroundings, each effect they produce
on one another, results directly and exclusively from active use of muscle
on the part of each separate individual. But some of the most minimal of
bodily activities produce the maximum effects. Physical cues produced
by one individual heavily influence others' behavior. Human individuals
cannot alone much change their surroundings. They have each, by
themselves, a negligible influence on nature. But the direct and indirect
effects on other individuals of what they do can make their doings matter
enormously in nature.

Those human bodily performances that attract the attention of the doer's peers no doubt produce a more profound and powerful effect than any other physical exertions of the individual. The subtlest movements exceed the most strenuous in their potency, for they carry social stimuli. Yet such activities acquire a social function and significance solely through reactions to them on the part of other human beings. Acute awareness of the postures, expressions, and adornments of the bodies of communicative partners in given contexts equips a human being to participate in complex, systematic interchanges of displays—communicative acts of all kinds—that structure social enterprise and through it transform the environment and habitat.

Many kinds of creatures, of course, pay heed to other members of their species and interact with them frequently. However, the social integration thus fostered has reached a particularly high level in the human species. Extremely frequent close interaction and diverse collaborative enterprise involving several individuals characterize all known human populations and far exceed the coordinated common efforts of other mammals. The social insects, in fact, seemingly provide the closest parallel, although they employ dissimilar and utterly rigid mechanisms of display and so lack humanity's spontaneity and versatility.

The maintenance and management of such intensive sociality rest upon persistent mutual monitoring among all individuals, as well as profuse performance of displays, that is, activities expressly directed toward communicative effects. And those displays can inspire imitation and instigate cooperation.

In what way do human beings cooperate among themselves? Still only in using their bodies. Then how do numbers of people coordinate that use of their bodies? Again through bodily means. They perform displays, which means that they not only show off significant objects but also speak and make gestures. And they watch and listen intently, taking their major cues from their fellows' displays of bodily movements, even as subtle as those forming speech. They also need to invoke other clues implanted in their physical surroundings. Employing such means, they engage in the formalized, reciprocating performances, described in the chapters to follow, that regulate their common undertakings. These patterns of activity have developed on the basis of evolved organic features of the human body and mind and most likely rest on genetic inheritance, as the instance of Williams' Syndrome indicates.

Transactions with environment involve mechanical relationships and processes. Any creature with a body functions as a mechanical agent in nature. Its structure determines and limits its manner of adaptation. Accordingly, the human body can do things only because of its physical character. Often likened to a machine, it operates as a particular mechanical system of rather modest capacities. It commands only slight energy supplies of its own. Varied sensory devices enable it, however, to apply its energies in a highly sensitive and selective manner. It readily examines and observes, experiments and manipulates. Thus it can perform its mechanical tasks with considerable precision. In this respect, however, the human constitution differs very little from that of many other creatures. But its unusually versatile "frontal field" of upper limbs and sensory organs endows it with special advantages, and I shall maintain that those latter derive mostly from heightened display capabilities. More important, though, a probably innate and also inveterate tendency to imitate, to imitate eagerly and faithfully and enduringly, sets humans apart.

Imitation is one way of learning. A very protracted learning process, essential for success even in a life of hunting and gathering, in itself prepares the human individual to deal with nature on more favorable terms and also presupposes a closely knit, communicating social group. But within humanity, particularly, learning from peers continues life long, much influenced by active example, coaching, and teaching. The constant communicative bombardment of individuals by diffusive information enables people to go on all their lives absorbing and incorporating new routines of activity from their fellows and often profiting from them. It also coordinates social activity. Such is the core of the human ecological program.

Human livelihood technologies do depend, unmistakably, in the end upon communication. The ecological reasons for this fact are not hard to discover and in fact are well known. The somatic characteristics and impinging ecological conditions that together govern human welfare and survival produce their joint effects indirectly, rather than through an immediate and intimate relationship of each individual with a pristine natural habitat. Interactions with nature are buffered both by intervening artificial circumstances created by human labor and by concerted collective enterprise and care dependent on communication. And the latter two features require a relative freedom from spatial constraint.

A "territorial imperative," as Robert Ardrey (1966) called it, may well exist potentially for human beings as for many animals, but it has to yield before the greater urgency of natural necessity. An ecological imperative takes precedence, ordaining that survival for both individual and human group shall depend on widely ranging exploitation of resources and concerted labor, unimpeded by the petty bounds of guarded dwelling places. "Home sweet home"—but the grass is always greener on the other side of the fence, and we need it.

Transcendence over territoriality is what opens up the opportunity for humankind to grow and spread and take possession and transform the world. And as will become evident in what follows here, spatial—and also temporal—transcendence can only be achieved through appropriate communicative action. Human beings, by virtue of their very body size, must range and forage widely just to feed themselves, lacking any other reliably efficient way to wrest a livelihood from a reluctant habitat. The livelihood strategy exceeds the powers of an individual alone; the technologies required emerge as products of protracted and concerted action and of shared experience, as do their implements. And even a purely hunting and gathering existence evidently lies beyond the capacities of a human individual denied such shared experience and technological devices. Despite the persistent myth of the wolf-child, never fairly substantiated, human beings cannot last for long alone without at least a human upbringing and some artifacts.

The concatenated circulations within that most inclusive of spatial domains, the general global environment, exert an important effect on any organism's habitat and welfare. At the other extreme, the momentary exact location of a creature with respect to either prey and provender or predators, and also local weather conditions, weighs in its chances of survival and consequently in some tiny way on the prospects for continuation of its genes and its species. But sociality, culture, and collaboration mightily mitigate the direct impact of such environmental and habitat features.

Habitat is an explicitly ecological term. Ecologists investigate relationships between plants or animals and the rest of the contents and conditions of the living space. More specifically, those scientists scrutinize, measure, and model the dyanamics involved, the mutual interactions and influences operating between an organism and its surroundings. When attention thus concentrates on the living conditions of the organism, the area on which it focuses is being conceived as a habitat.

Human relationships with habitats exhibit almost as much particularity as do those established by animals and plants, unless so buffered and altered artificially that their rigors become assuaged. Communication, that is, specifically the imitative diffusion of activity routines and their products, contributes most to accomplishing that. Nonetheless, the processes of nature still in the end determine the basic conditions of life even for any human population. This truth, too long disregarded, has lately been forced to the fore in public awareness by the undeniable deterioration of many familiar habitats.

In many cases territoriality may circumscribe effective habitat. Among the spatial entities significant in the lives of either animals or people, defended residential territory necessarily takes precedence over all other arrangements. The home provides not alone defense against hostile intruders but protection as well from cold and heat and rain, and in very uneven degree some level of hygiene to guard against disease. Defense and protection extend to possessions as well, and home furthermore furnishes a favored place for learning and teaching. The security and salubrity of the several home territories making up the mosaic of occupation of an area therefore matter enormously for mammals, birds, reptiles, and human beings alike. But humanity's means of suspending spatial restrictions endow it with additional spatial attributes wherein the human species stands apart. As subsequent chapters will detail, they reflect its peculiar ways of communication.

First among the consequences of communication for humanity, then, ranks ecological advantage for the species as a whole. It derives from the spatially organized cooperation moderating nature's harshness, penuriousness, and inconstancy. In contrast, however, to the normal approximate equality of living conditions among the animal territories in a single vicinity, the marked inequalities that exist among the homes and possessions and livelihoods of people in a given place are induced precisely by communicative action within those same spatial frameworks that structure cooperation.

Circulation of goods and imitation of techniques do compensate for habitat insufficiencies, but highly unevenly. Like the birds that range widely collecting tidbits to take to their nestlings, human beings in the simplest cultural state may simply forage in a similar way and carry back what they can to the camp. Obviously, though, most people's living conditions depend but slightly on what they might outright gather from the wild. Various kinds of social exchange intervene in most instances between the individual and nature. Most of humanity must now buy and sell in order to live.

This dictate embroils individuals inextricably with extended social and spatial relationships and the physical facilities that embody them. The placement of people within the immense complexity of such a total spatial system tends firmly to determine their possibilities of action and their access to both influence and income.

This essay argues that the genetic program of the human species has somehow evolved in such a manner as to permit a peculiar development of human communicative behavior. Certain yet unidentified genes, it maintains, selected and perpetuated through time, must account for the collaborative and also competitive capabilities, and hence the spatial dispositions and the technological effectiveness of the species, and therefore its capacities for modifying and expanding its environments. Humanity has thereby proved able to persist and proliferate vastly—but always acting at its own peril.

The animal body evolves and behavior must likewise change over time. Even human behavior suffers selection and shaping. Despite the present striking physical uniformity of this one ubiquitous species, individual practices vary, cultural contrasts are common, and dissimilar modified landscapes show the results. In itself, however, such human and geographical diversity need not stem directly from correspondingly different genetic endowments in various human communities.

In fact, the present argument runs the opposite way: a distinctive and uniform human communicative behavior pattern, involving competitive object and performance displays and their appropriation and repetition, produces observable human variety without requiring extensive genetic disparities within the species. As Peter C. Reynolds (1981) has convincingly suggested, the concept of culture merely describes this result; by itself, it does not explain it.

This essay in fact will argue, perhaps paradoxically, that people differ so much because they are everywhere so much alike. Our common, universal human features make us what we are; and even cultural diversity appears really no more than their understandable consequence in any fair biological sense. Humanity interacts and interbreeds as one single species and, nowadays, nearly as just one community. It is more than plausible to suppose that our very genetic variation, competitively fostered by the differential in reproductive success among genes, still steers the evolution of the species always toward some kind of unity, instead of giving rise to new, dissimilar species.

The unmistakable worldwide sameness of the human behavioral program, in particular of the universal patterns of communication, can probably account for all substantial difference in the species. If that is not enough of a paradox, then consider the following point.

Human beings collaborate so effectively and modify their world so much precisely because of the way they compete. As Thorstein Veblen (1918) and a succession of subsequent skeptical writers have pointed out, human beings tend to "show off" in competition for notice and influence and will frequently sacrifice seemingly more practical considerations on behalf of impressions they make. The immediate, highly practical prize is quite other than livelihood security or even direct genetic predominance. It is what I call Geltung.

I shall contend that human behavior responds universally to the interpersonal effectiveness in communication that I have termed Geltung and that the latter reflects a specific feature acquired through evolutionary selection. Everyone seeks it and suffers the stress that goes with the search for it. And personal Geltung, achieved through admittedly competitive communicative display, assures social collaboration, spatial openness, and cultural initiative and influence to those who can manifest it. Geltung adapts the individual, adapts the species, and itself adapts to the habitat; and individuals attempt to adapt their behavior and even surroundings in ways propitious for personal Geltung.

The circumstance of having to use an unfamiliar German word, in the absence of a good equivalent in English, no doubt has lent a little mystery to the foregoing assertion. What would have done: Reputation? Respect? Legitimacy? Validity? Worth? Esteem? Acceptance? Authority? Credibility? Counting for something? Mattering to other people? Being "somebody"?

All those terms can help define Geltung, and yet others might be equally pertinent. Put them all together and maybe you get an inkling of its scope. But the imported, "made in Germany" word is a much superior precision instrument, if you're not too rabid a linguistic protectionist.

Thus the Geltung (pronounced as the "gel-" of "gelding" and then "-toong") of a person, a thing, or an action (action is really what measures it) has no certainty attaching to it. All is not always as it appears, and Geltung concerns appearances. It may well mask feigning and falsification. Therefore I introduce the term here to recognize simply a set of dimensions against which to judge the "self-presentations" made by people. Yet more to the point, I shall go on to ask the reader to regard these dimensions as singularly apt as indicators of what guides behavior and responses to it. Thus I use "Geltung" in the sense of the relative magnitudes of certain qualities attributed to individuals in and by discourse or action in general.

The inveterate and universal human practice of cultivating appearances in order to cultivate people meets its perpetual test in the kind and degree of Geltung it yields. Serving to influence people, hence Geltung discharges political functions, however badly or well. In fact, attention to Geltung and to its effects reveals a pervasive political element in most human action, for politics consists after all of the differential exercise of influence.

Dale Carnegie wrote a best-selling book called *How to Win Friends and Influence People*. Embarrassingly corny as it might appear now, that book of his addressed a matter that people were eager to know about, and his folksy prescriptions often hit home. In essence, he wrote about Geltung without ever knowing it. And so did Thorstein Veblen, for instance, and any number of others—even, in their own way, Dante and Shakespeare and Goethe and Tolstoy.

They all dwelt on the fact that people are important to everyone and therefore worth cultivating. All these and countless other authors, however, also took note of the familiar human propensity to cultivate appearances as well, precisely as a means of dealing with people. Writers and philosophers have viewed that inclination variously, as everything from legitimate pride and enlightened self-advancement to folly and vanity. The "wisdom" books of the Bible, for instance, devote much critical emphasis to these persistent human attributes, and some of the most renowned Persian poetry and Chinese classical books read the same way.

Who can draw exact dividing lines between wisdom and prudence, on the one hand, and calculation and guile, on the other? What distinguishes self-esteem and dignity from pomp and vainglory? Questions of this sort, when asked about persons themselves—their character and personality—invite *ad hominem* judgments, but such are not the questions here. What count are active responses to actions. Emphasis in this discussion will focus, accordingly, on manifest reactions to manifest actions. The argument emphasizes how certain personal displays provoke and promote either a positive or a negative, a favorable or unfavorable response, or none at all. It will interpret such response as either threatening or discouraging, or else reassuring and heartening. And it will seek to assess the implications by asserting the extreme, the vital importance of those displays and especially of reactions to them by other people.

This position requires a positive stand on the merits of persistent "self-presentation," which Erving Goffman brilliantly dissected in some of his books (1967, 1970, 1971). The paragraph above in fact extolled its "extreme . . . vital importance." After all, hardly anyone would quarrel with the proposition that people are important and that cultivating them through presenting a proper appearance is often legitimate and desirable, even if it has limits. Display designed to influence others, if not always to cultivate them, constitutes a vital part of what we might call the animal heritage of human beings.

Modern ethologists and nature photographers have provided voluminous and conclusive evidence that during their day even carnivorous beasts display their often fearsome armaments more frequently as threats among themselves than they use them in actual fighting or indeed catching food. Human beings, lacking such intimidating adornments, have to proceed otherwise. The comprehensive panoply of public appearance, ourselves entire on display, not our fangs or our claws, is the mightiest weapon we have. We try to keep it well sharpened. But ideally we use it to cooperate, in a somewhat competitive manner, rather than to kill or to hurt. Human communication amounts to a curious kind of cooperation that serves competition within the species and competes for survival in nature through fostering additional cooperation.

On earth, we suppose, only people truly have selves; we presume, perhaps rather hastily, that no other animal does. The selves of humanity function as organs like others; their role is adaptive, as that of bodily organs in animals is or has been. That feature is no accident, by today at any rate, although its history must have begun with chance genetic mutations that natural selection in the long run vindicated conclusively.

The self consists not alone of the body but likewise of all that the functioning body displays and of all the impressions the body and its displays together make on that bodily individual's awareness. Its counterpart within the awareness of our fellows we can call the "persona" or simply the person. The presentation of the self through display, or more accurately its public depiction as a person, unmistakably constitutes a normal and necessary aspect of human activity. Apart from those primitive urges, universal among sentient creatures, to which the injunction "fight or flee" corresponds, it figures, in all probability, as the object of some of our dearest and deepest motivations. That driver of action may often escape immediate awareness, but it coils down there inside us like a watch spring, even somehow "out of mind," wound up and ready to drive us to communicate. It seems to be what makes us tick, and talk, and show off.

When rebuffed by responses their displays elicit from their fellows, however, people feel pain and alarm and seek some remedy. And whenever the reaction to some display seems positive, the individual thrives on the reassurance and support received. An ensuing section will consider the relevance to this argument of the psychological impact of manifest approval and disapproval, the states of shame and guilt, satisfaction with self and elation, that all of us know in ourselves.

What underlies such reactions? What do most people want out of life? Was Alexander Pope right when he wrote the following lines?

Happy the man whose wish and care
A few paternal acres bound,
Content to breathe his native air
In his own ground.

Peace and contentment may do for the few, but it mostly appears that the many want fame, wealth, and power and run after fashion. Or in contrast are friendship and love the most coveted prizes, perhaps? Or perchance does a person long to be useful, accepting the dictum of Goethe in his *Iphigenie* that "a useless life is an early death"?

Presumably any and all of those "fair advantages" gratify those who can earn them. Geltung both attaches to any of them, opening doors and widening opportunities, and beforehand makes it easier for them to be achieved. Geltung begets further Geltung. It accomplishes more, far more, to be sure, providing support and encouragement to worthy undertakings, but on occasion likewise to ignoble or fatuous deeds as well.

A Latin proverb says that virtue is its own reward, and that is a lofty conception. However, virtue acclaimed or alleged is more to the taste of most people than any secret merit might be, and its potent diffusing distillate, reputation, much eases their progression and affairs. Such Geltung affords them entry and influence, welcome and trust.

Celebrity and popularity may carry their costs, but their heady appeal is seductively hard to disdain. Their insidious fascination all too readily overcomes a person's realistic vigilance against self-deception. The power in society that they confer too often becomes an end in itself, corrupting and blinding. Moreover, the attribution of virtue, whatever its basis, can yield material gains, and these, however misplaced, perhaps can seem even more irresistible.

The supposed gratifications listed above surely do matter to people but appear as no more than the crudest clue to the fullness of inner desire. The next chapter discusses how, propelled by something internal, communication seeks for responses and employs them to establish Geltung.

TWO

• Provocation Produces Results

"The wheel that does the squeaking gets the grease." Provocation produces results. Human communication, as herein portrayed, always seeks some response. It serves to elicit results of importance or interest to the interlocutors, who challenge, charm, cajole, entice, exhort, inspire, intimidate, and otherwise maneuver to get their opposites to act in particular ways.

Remember the hippies? Liberated spirits that they were, they freed themselves from the fetters of bourgeois conformity and custom. "Drop out, tune in, turn on" went their motto, and their colonies lived it with hearty conviction. Acrid smoke, strident new music, and foodstuffs they never would touch back home filled their disorderly dens.

Yes, colonies! Spontaneous, independent, and creative, the hippies flocked and huddled together as if they were nothing but sheep of another strange variety. Beards and long locks looked identical throughout the whole movement; it was hard for the layperson to tell one "freak" from the others. Hippie tribes unanimously dressed in long skirts and blue denim and uniformly shod themselves in sandals or went barefoot. How odd that freedom and nonconformity would always wear the identical badges!

It doesn't take feathers (though some hippies fancied them) in order to flock together; but it does take something equivalent, just the same. People have to display if they wish to be noticed at all. Everyone yearns irrepressibly for inclusion in some kind of community, and the displays that people present, soliciting Geltung, determine the welcome received. Without accepting some standards of Geltung, a person just cannot belong.

Belonging fosters nice cozy feelings, but that is hardly the half of it. The real prescription reads more like "belong, but then, too, get along." Within any circle of associates, important or trivial transactions go on all the time and have to be conducted with some degree of agreement and mutual aid. The dropouts of the sixties and seventies discovered that they still must develop enough accord among themselves to coexist and cooperate—or even to quarrel productively.

Does Geltung guarantee harmony, then? Not at all! Concord comes only with labor and luck. But Geltung does do things less merciful but more important. It not only serves for much more than the first indispensable provocation, and in fact even negative Geltung suffices for that. What, and how well, a person displays carries much weight both in extracting information in general from interlocutors and in eliciting particular kinds of responses indicated likewise in observable behavior.

Always relative, recall, the Geltung attaching to one individual's display exerts its effect exclusively as a function of comparison with that of the interlocutor or of some other exemplar. Nobody ever can manifest unqualified, incomparable, absolute Geltung. Hence the results of display interactions tend to reflect a differential in personal Geltung disclosed by some feature inherent in the momentary net display. The implications of this fact are well known to off-duty police wearing civil attire.

Surroundings—the venue—count too, of course. Every act has its own proper possible venues, which shadow potential success. The venue always takes part in the total display. A judge cannot pronounce sentence away from the court.

Now imagine some things that displays can accomplish, aside from attracting attention and opening dialog, provided their authors can muster a Geltung advantage.

Without exception a display invites information in the reply—something novel. The report received can consist only of something about the one who responds, but it may say much more as a consequence. This claim may appear improbable: do we not obtain information concerning the world and the state of things in it from dialog? No, we do not—not directly, that is, beyond one class of uncertain particulars. Another person can tell you nothing that is completely impersonal. Every utterance betrays a personal touch, everyone speaks or acts from some private angle or bias. Any statement comes from a standpoint. Hence an assertion concerning even the weather, the right road to Rome, or the state of the stock market says a little bit as well about whoever expressed it. The whole person talks.

Interlocutors might sometimes check up on what they are told, to be sure, by requiring material evidence. But veracity is not the issue here; there exists no absolute veracity, perhaps, beyond whatever might lie in the largely unverifiable claims about themselves that people make. And how misleading those can be!

Dialog garners and gives information, colored and filtered by private presupposition and prejudice, but can never attain to complete objectivity. At most it can fish for plausible answers, mostly taken on faith but susceptible always to testing. Interlocutors can choose to continue simply to investigate or "problematize," in whatever manner they like, until satisfied.

Probably, apart from the great mass of provisionally acceptable conjectures about the world at large, responding displays mostly comment on the state of the individuals who proffer them. The assessment of these answers, too, remains a fully subjective matter. The interlocutors must gauge one another's responses however they will. And still, the procedure works well enough.

A person can commonly observe the signs that reveal that the dialog partner has been delighted, distracted, or deceived; entranced or encouraged; intimidated or infuriated; intrigued, inspired to imitate, or spurred to some other initiative. Responses offer indications of whether a display has reassured or alarmed or otherwise troubled, flattered, or outraged the other party.

The range of responses received is much wider than those just suggested, of course, and individuals differ in both their ability to incite them and their own acuity in sensing effects they produce. The exceptional sensitivity of canny traders and fortune tellers in this regard is legendary, as is also the obtuseness of dullards, dupes, and bores.

In any case, immediate reactions of those kinds are seldom sought for their own sake. They lead the dialog toward further ends and results. And although, as a subsequent section maintains, many such outcomes primarily serve the enhancement of personal Geltung, additional, utterly different determinants also underlie deeply the actions of people, including communicative exchanges.

Humanity does not live by bread alone, certainly, and also not for Geltung exclusively. The foregoing forceful advocacy ought not to obscure the fact that certain other needs lie much deeper. The urge to express, and to seek information thereby, is only one among the fundamental tendencies of exploration, experiment, and advance or evasion that program organisms for survival. When response to inquiring displays does not establish conviction, an individual may switch over into another mode and take recourse to independent investigation—exploring or experimenting or just waiting to verify the proffered claim. This demonstrates nicely that something deeper than Geltung guards against falsehood.

Creatures as inconspicuous as microbes or mosses reach out to test their environments and respond according to what they discover. Their skin or integument does more than hold bodily contents in. It engages directly with the outside world and participates in it, transmitting information gained along to the being inside it. Animal mobility aids in this quest; active exploration of environment facilitates finding out things of importance. The sense organs, also, function not passively but in active search for information. The bodily extremities permit a creature to indulge in experiment, too, especially when endowed with prehensile capabilities. In any living thing, a hunger for information burns fully as strongly as hunger for nourishment. Just watch a wild tiger's cautious approach to a bait!

The fight-or-flee reaction that animals show regulates itself in part by means of this wary alertness. Approach or retreat depend on it. Human beings, as much as any other living creatures, crave information before proceeding to action. "Look before you leap." "You'd better watch what you're getting into!"

But people do not always pause and search and watch before acting, any more than they always assemble their Geltung in display. Emotional surges eclipse that preoccupation in favor of others more inward and intimate. Human beings can get carried away, lost in their work or amusements, oblivious to all impressions produced. Curiosity, the keynote of staying alive, can obliterate social restraint. Compassion, the glory of living as human, can magnify social concern far beyond matters of Geltung.

In all but a few human beings, Geltung considerations yield priority to nobler ones: integrity, artistry, workmanship, creativity, charity, love, loyalty, and esthetic delight. *Joie de vivre* does not describe the life led in fearful courting of good impressions. Deep down, the self that lives with the self knows what matters.

It cannot escape the reader's notice that some of these paragraphs proclaim the importance of the superficial side of human behavior. But wait! We can only see what appears on the surface of things. We intuit what happens inside, and always unsurely. The holiest hermits, deprived of all comfort and company, alone in their deserts incapable of doing visible wrong, reportedly suffered over their sins. Conversely, honored presidents and trusted priests secretly perpetrate unseemly deeds. All the Geltung in the world cannot entirely vouch for true virtue, wisdom, or strength, and much of the prudence, justice, temperance, and fortitude existing in this world will earn no Geltung at all.

Literary works in virtually all languages describe countless examples of Geltung pursuit and the folly of its excesses, in novels and dramas and poetry; scriptures and histories abound in similar testimonies. Alternatively, television and the daily papers provide far, far more than adequate coverage of it. Such vivid illustrations only lack the natural rationale of ecological fitness and communicative procedures that this book attempts to present.

Let it be admitted, then, that superficialities in human existence—surface appearances, to be exact—claim the major attention throughout this book. The esssay attempts to convey the understanding, however, that human beings have developed out of this feature a prime device for survival, unexcelled in the kingdoms of nature. With this due declaimer, now, discussion returns to the workings of Geltung.

If love is not really blind, it is surely accepting and comforting. To be loved is to matter intensely to someone, to enlist a witness to one's ostensible worth and virtues in spite of the rest of the world's opinion. Love awards lavish Geltung, in bulk and on faith, richly and rashly and unreservedly. A mother's love is best of all. How often one hears that only a mother could love someone especially ugly or disreputable! Fatherly love by comparison seems demanding and almost grudging. In many cultures, the mother-figure rightfully commands more devotion and praise than any other by far. Whom can you trust if not your own mother?

Romantic love still embroils nearly everyone once in a while despite the doubts and pangs that poets are wont to bemoan. Disdaining to fix on the traits in a person most regarded by the rest of the world, this love attaches to minutiae in look and manner that appear to other people altogether unremarkable. No word do the poets employ more frequently than "love," and no greater authorities exist than they when it comes to its inspirations. However, no poets have ever, at least to my knowledge, sung of love born of practicality or prudence. Dramatists often illustrate the willfulness of love, the way it spurns orderly cultivation. It springs up where it will, more like a weed than a crop. Love is a wildness.

The poets seldom extol their lover's cash balance or committee chair-manship. Such unimaginable praise would chill the heart and kill the love of the dear one—although surely not always incapable of sparking desire. A scrupulous keeping to standards other than success or posses-sion allows a lover to allay the pains and fears attending ordinary life and exalts the person alone. Sparing and spoiling their opposites a little, lov-ers make addicts out of them. Generous Geltung flows freely. Only that fact makes comprehensible the choices people make in love.

Granting an important distinction between love and marriage, one must still regard them both as bulwarks against an uncaring and overly judgmental world. Love and a happy marriage make more of a home than the rest of the world can provide.

What if illusion be called the essence of love? That simply alludes to a high form of faith—an unconditioned commitment. And illusion differs from delusion or deception. Although both of that pair of falsehoods have regularly wormed their way into the apple of love ever since Eve and the serpent spoiled Eden, the promise of bliss still as always bedazzles the innocent. Even false love is sustaining until it gets unmasked. Fools' Geltung looks nearly real.

Fame, wealth, and power always seem to figure as primary sources and assurances of Geltung. However even these enviable attributes notori-ously do not invariably set to rest the craving for love's simple and secure acceptance. Celebrities have been known to demean themselves by in-sincerely exploiting the romantic dreams of youthful victims. Unattrac-tive or elderly moneybags shamelessly squander fortunes and reputations in troubled pursuit of the kind of love the poor take almost for granted. Squalid dalliances frequently imperil the careers of able politicians. How much belongs to love, indeed, and how much to lust, and what just to vanity? Many of the seekers are too old or vain to know.

Friendship constitutes another haven from worldly disdain and de-preciation, another sweet fountain of Geltung. You can tell things to a real friend that you wouldn't tell even to mother or lover. Once com-radely trust has been granted, almost anything goes but betrayal of loy-alty or confidence. Friendship rests less on bodily graces and traits than does love, and more perhaps upon character. It does have its practical side, too. Ability often wins friends. And friends stand by one another and help if they can in emergencies—something that lovers may do or may not. "A friend in need is a friend indeed."

Spurned tenders of friendship not merely injure pride but also can diminish a person's Geltung in the world's eyes. That is the deadliest trap for the social climber. The world regards unrequited love with more charity, although the incurable romantic always sighing over the unattainable seems foolish or weak. And forlorn is the word for the friendless.

"To thine own self be true," counseled Polonius. Some people at times get into a spot where nothing but being resolutely and defiantly themselves becomes conceivable. Placed in such a fateful position (notice the spatial allusion), they take their firm stand, like Martin Luther before the Imperial tribunal declaring, "Ich kann nicht anders"—I cannot do otherwise.

"Mine honor is my life; both grow in one; / Take honor from me, and my life is done," says Mowbray, Earl of Norfolk, in *King Richard II*. The life he speaks of is certainly not the mere life of the body, but that of the person enshrined in a self that the body but serves. Something more precious than physical life can endure: call it honor, reputation, or if you will, the ideal image of the self or its Geltung. Yet it may well attract no attention or praise; those are irrelevant. It has to assume a determination to sacrifice, even in total obscurity, with little hope of remembrance. Honor is antithetical to surface show.

Honor—which, to be sure, constitutes no more than one guise of Geltung—takes on varied expressions yet always calls for lonely courage, inner discipline, and self-determination. It never quails before the shouting of a crowd, nor qualifies its words to please. It plants its roots in responsibilities—to the self and family name, to the nation, to comrades, to some divine power—and correspondingly reveals itself in varied places and circumstances. Honor furthermore partakes of the nature of loyalty, faith, and probity at once, and each of its most dramatic demonstrations centers on one or more of these virtues of everyday heroes.

Heroes and martyrs are kin. The Iroquois warrior scornful under torture upheld the same honor as the soldier saving comrades at the cost of dying; alike they are heroes. Giordano Bruno, burned by the Catholic Inquisition for his science, shared the fate of the saints of that very Church, burned at the stake for their faith; all were martyrs.

Similar determined sacrifice in many cultures makes saints and sends them to heaven, whether as Muslim militants who perish gladly in a jihad, Buddhist arhats liberated from materiality, or Christian hermits slowly dessicated on their pillars in the desert.

Many a lesser but still costly sacrifice is made every day by individuals who testify to truth before power. Jails and concentration camps confine a host of such stubborn champions of honesty. So much as truly disclosing one's ethnic or confessional identity, normally a matter of pride, can be fatal. The Holocaust, the slaughter after Partition in India, the ruthless persecution of the Baha'i in modern Iran, Serb ethnic cleansing—all proclaim the possible costs of being oneself.

Nevertheless, we find the heroic response comprehensible. Anyone may have to take a fatal stand in defense of something; if not of honor and faith, at least of family or friends. And most people recoil from outright disloyalty or duplicity. The very thieves have their honor of sorts. The redoubtable Mafia, even, lives by its absolute code of *omertà*. Geltung or honor somewhere draws a defiant line.

The stubborn refusal to conform and capitulate, distinguishing the hero and martyr, thus also appears among criminals. To be sure, the iniquitous invention of a special category of so-called political crimes admits that what counts as virtue in one country may figure as crime in another. Moreover, even obedient agents of terror and torture carry out their monstruous mission in complacent professional ways, bound together by pernicious pride and loyalty to their collaborators, if not to their nominal masters. What else but a warped form of Geltung could explain their cruelty and pitiless callousness?

A sociobiologist might well point out that stalwart adherence to being oneself—regardless of any moral evaluations—may in the long run of evolution favor perpetuation of the individual's genetic stock. The phenomenon of territoriality mentioned above, so widely found among animals, provides a fair instance of how a determined stand even when confronting superior strength can dissuade aggression and protect the kindred group.

Being oneself implies choice. It is hard to conceive of such choice without freedom. Sacrifice shows that human freedom is real.

Insects, we imagine, are not free beings. In terms of a general theory of information, we might say that insect communication confines itself approximately to identity or "station" signals and displays among totally determinate agents. Even their mode of self-sacrifice is like that of a mindless automaton, as far as we know.

Human communication, on the other hand, can report on a great variety of additional, unforetold particulars and may falsify as readily as tell the truth. It can discuss the past or the future, and anything distant or mythical, too. It knows how to abstract. Its informational content is immeasurably richer on account of the incomparably greater freedom of individual response. Such communication holds the key to human freedom.

The respective freedoms of speech, religion, assembly, and press enshrined in the American Bill of Rights, for example, consist of protection for unrestricted utterance. Ideally, they entitle individuals to say and display whatever they like. Corresponding rights are defined in the charters, constitutions, or statutes of most nations today, whether or not they are honored. In addition, though, the absolute necessity of freedom follows from the very character of human dialog.

Information always means novelty, and communication always means a flow of information. Although ants and bees, for instance, obviously interact among themselves in active search for information, they do so presumably by a form of exploration rather than the genuine expressive provocation that characterizes human beings, other mammals, and birds, for example. Only the latter cases, then, truly represent free communication embodying an aleatory highly contingent individual response. (The insects do not really ask; they simply test or scan.) In human communication, the novelty imparted by the interlocutor can exist only because the party addressed enjoys a free choice of response; if that response were determined in advance or unvaryingly standardized, no novelty and hence no information would be transmitted and no true communication would take place. That, of course, is why we cannot really communicate with inanimate objects, even mighty computers, no matter how well they may simulate genuinely free responses, or crib their answers from their programmers. If genuine "thinking" computers do ever emerge, it will mean that they have acquired internal autonomous means of exercising a freedom comparable to that of people. (Will they then have emotions?)

Although human communication, as one form of inquiry, does resemble experimentation, such as that which instructs us so much about the physical world, it differs notably from experiment in that we cannot treat the human response, as we do that of inanimate objects, even computers, as totally determinate. In contrast, science could garner no principles from testing nature if nature could choose to respond in a different way each time retested.

Subsequent chapters will describe the procedures universally employed in human dialog and indicate where free response must enter into them. Obviously, however, those procedures by no means establish or ensure total freedom for human beings. This species, like any other, lives under close and inflexible natural constraints, although it has admittedly found ways of abating or mitigating a number of them. Scientists and other people tend to refer to those conditions of nature that they see no prospect of changing as "natural laws," and to seek security and power for humanity in trying to obey and apply them as closely as possible, with considerable success at that. But whatever exemption or easement that results is attained on the whole through disciplined, collective endeavor, which itself introduces new constraints. We acknowledge that human life in fact is lived in a tension between freedom and constraint.

The freedom invoked in communication counts for something just because it punctuates a fixed, derminate, and hence constraining routine of interaction. You cannot play chess without pieces and board, even if only imagined. Nevertheless, in chess as in life, both the character of the stimuli responding to an interlocutor's challenge and the medium through which those stimuli are delivered may vary freely. In abstract terms, we might say that the choice of communication channels or media, as well as the "message" or utterance transmitted, remains completely open and elective, but that both elements acquire significance only within the respective procedural and technical frameworks imposed by the total constraining communication system.

The acts of display alluded to so frequently above now require more analysis.

THREE

• Acts of Display

I live in the beautiful land of the potlatch, British Columbia, Canada. Here, amid "the murmuring pines and the hemlocks," stood once along the shores the great plank houses of the Tsimshian, Haida, Kwagiulth, and Nutka clans and the equally big, Quonset-like dwellings of Salishan peoples. These gifted indigeneous folk had developed not only their now world-renowned arts but also a sturdy livelihood strategy, based on the sea and highly complex social systems. They also celebrated sumptuous orgies of display.

How could a person living in this blessed province and aware of the aboriginal inhabitants' achievements and dignities not sooner or later come upon the concept of Geltung? The indigenous peoples would have grasped it forthwith.

These Northwest Coast nations maintained their stratified societies, and managed interpersonal rivalries, in part through the lavish ceremonials called potlatches. Cruelly suppressed until recently by government agents and highly intolerant missionaries, these gatherings have now been revived, and the confiscated impedimenta are slowly being reclaimed by their owners from museums and distant private collections.

The keynotes of potlatch were pride and prodigality, along with exquisite etiquette. On such occasions as name-giving ceremonials, marriages, accessions to rank, or funerals, these quintessential rites of passage assembled the community and honored guests at a lavish feast of barbecued salmon, fishy eulachon grease, a frothy wild berry dessert, and other traditional delights. The company had to listen to lengthy oratorical professions of personal importance, as well as receive generous gifts gathered from all the clan and distributed, with somewhat invidious undertones, by the celebrants. Some among the most precious objects brought forth were haughtily cast down into the sea as testimonials of grandeur.

Drawing its wealth from the kinship network wherever dispersed, a successful potlatch display would broadcast both the fame and the lavish presents of its givers around the whole constellation of small seaside villages and fishing encampments far up and down the rain-washed coast. It conferred political power, solidifying and extending the influence of the giver, humiliating rivals, and cementing alliances.

A pioneer French sociologist, Marcel Mauss (1954), pointed out how presents bind people together, but he also showed that a gift can be less than a bargain. In North American business firms, a gold watch says "goodbye, and don't hurry back." The Japanese, probably the world's most obsessive gift givers, live in terror of finding themselves unable to reciprocate, with interest, for whatever they are given. With acceptance goes obligation; we still say "much obliged" for small favors. Surely the potlatch could impose an onerous, indeed crushing and shameful obligation on an impoverished guest, but it likewise had a more positive, benevolent, and less competitive side. The anthropologist Helen Codere no doubt went too far in calling it "fighting with goods." In general the opulent, highly dramatic ceremonial may leave someone offended or injured, but that is not the main aim. It served to integrate the society.

The potlatch has had numerous counterparts in ceremonials around the world and in history. A few examples will illuminate the possibilities inherent in large-scale Geltung display. Consider the case of the Maya. This group of Central American nations was formerly lauded as peaceful and mild, but all that has changed since archaeologist Tatiana Proskouriakoff began to decipher the glyphs, the Mayan system of writing inscribed on great stelae (tall standing tablets of stone) and carved into building façades. What she and her successors found were histories of bellicose, fierce little states that reveled in capturing and sacrificing each others' nobles and kings, though probably not the commoners. They practiced decapitation and torture on a nauseating scale, as better comprehension of their exquisite pictorial carvings has finally brought home to their formerly uncritical admirers. Understandably, the literature dealing with these peoples has recently assumed an entirely new tone.

However, the Maya could not have practiced cruelty for its own sake alone. The solemn sacrificial events the stones portray, no doubt like heretic-burning in Europe holding religious significance, conformed to the Mayan cultures, and certainly the rulers could grasp their implications for themselves. Nobody takes on a kingship or presidency even today without a real risk, for that is just part of the game. An unfortunate high-born Mayan lord, slated for sacrifice, might moreover take consolation and some satisfaction from the very opportunity for the equanimity and contempt with which he underwent the ministrations of the executioners. Scornful stoicism under torment was always an ornament the equal of any other proud display.

Many indigenous people around the globe (e.g., the Iroquois and Maori) have practiced analogous bloodthirsty ceremonials and still permitted the victims tortured or otherwise sacrificed to claim their own share of glory through defiant impassivity. Yet the model offered by the potlatch helps to make sense of a host of other ceremonials of glory not enacted in blood, or at least not involving human victims. The native nations of the North American Prairies and Great Plains, although sometimes addicted to stealthy raiding designed to capture enemy prizes of anything from horses to women or scalps, by predilection "counted coup," as the French explorers put it: to the proud acclaim of the tribe, the proficient brave would tally up the number of times he had crept up and touched an enemy warrior, and then escaped alive.

The triumphs of the Roman emperors returning from their campaigns; the Southeast Asian "feasts of honor," centering on the ritual sacrifice of prized indigenous cattle; the periodic visit of the Tenno, the emperor of Japan, to converse with and placate the gods at the great shrine of Ise; and a large variety of other splendid, but often highly wasteful, public observances resemble the potlatch in character and function. But even small private acts of display serve the same ends.

Have you ever watched a peacock parade the gorgeous fan of its feathers? Did you never recoil from a dog displaying its threatening teeth? All human beings also display, and not simply their feathers or teeth, nor out of their vanity. When they communicate, they display in support of their personal Geltung. How do they do so?

The communication systems used by humanity differ in diversity and versatility but not, I contend, altogether in kind, from those employed by the more advanced of the animals, invertebrates as well as vertebrates. What do people display, and why and how do they do it? We can approach those questions by noticing first some general features of typical animal display behavior.

The term "display," proposed by W. John Smith (1977) to cover all communicative animal behavior, conjures up lavish exhibitions of color, movement, or sound, and this description sometimes fits the actuality. In particular, the courtship displays (we have them, too!) of certain species attain extravagant and bizarre forms, such as the exuberant nuptial dances of various species of birds and the polychromatic love shows of squids. Some large ungulates perform truly titanic combats that contest for mating priority. The connection with courtship ought to alert the observer to the role that display plays in breeding success, and thus in perpetuating particular genomes. However, the implications extend far beyond courtship itself and are not lost on humanity.

The cases just cited are rather extreme, however. Most species' display behavior involves only modest vocalizations, gestures, and postures or exceedingly minor habitat modifications. Yet display among human beings obviously includes a good deal more, suggesting its deep and far-reaching involvement in individual survival and net reproductive success.

The spectacular energy often discharged in the course of some animal displays, and their tendency at times to burst forth without evident cause, might suggest that they achieve little more than giving vent to intense internal pressures. And no doubt they do result from particular inner states and processes in the individual concerned. But the ecological and evolutionary function of any given display far exceeds the level of a simple easing of tensions or a gratification of internal longings. The tensions and longings, however pressing and genuine, arise in response to external stimuli, even if triggered simply by weather phenomena, and fit tightly into adaptive behavior.

Nature could not tolerate the cost of energy expended on such luxuries as mere comfort or pleasure for their own sakes. Thus display, like other behavior, must serve individual welfare or genetic survival while conserving resources and energy, whether or not in doing so it pleases the creature displaying.

Then in what concrete and specific way does survival-enhancing expressive display become manifest? Let us consult W. John Smith's conception. He holds communication to consist of an organism's deliberate emission of stimuli capable of influencing the behavior of another organism. This position implies a closed circuit of stimulus-response, in an exchange which of course may continue for any given period. Logically, it makes the presence, actual or potential, of a witness or hearer essential to the demonstration that communication is occurring.

In fact, no sort of true communication could operate for long as a one-way transmission lacking a possible response, and so any act of communication must ideally form one segment of a closed circuit. (This principle surely applies even to television, as will be explained subsequently.) On this account, it makes good sense to equate communicative action with an important class of explicitly interactive social performances, and expression with seeking response.

Expressly contradicting rival modern theories of communication, this principle in turn implies a relation among two and only two interlocutors—a dyad—as the fundamental unit of communication, although it allows for as many simultaneous dyadic receivers as a given transmission may reach. The one and only proof that communication is occurring is that which can be furnished by any specific respondent, but given the variety of respondents, a particular utterance—literally, letting something out—may produce varied effects and reactions in different recipients. Each case is distinctive and deserves a separate accounting, and any composite audience can be very diverse in its reactions. Professional communicators, such as advertisers and politicians, cannot afford to disregard that principle.

The candidate and publicist attempt to reach each and every potential adherent or customer. They try to please everyone, almost, but must tailor their pitch to the tastes of a varying multitude. Each hearer decides for herself or himself. A seller as well as a buyer has to beware.

Furthermore, something like presumption or boldness is often connoted by the word "display." We tend to look askance at show-offs and people who promote themselves too persistently. This aversion always haunts all display. The suggestiveness of the term does nevertheless echo an essential feature of display: its function is indeed necessarily provocative, a challenge to act.

Why must display inevitably be provocative? Recall that the relevant principle stipulates that, in order to count as communicative action, a display should not merely address a potential witness but should have the capability of evoking a response from that witness or "respondent." Hence it must by definition provoke or challenge. In other words, it furnishes a stimulus that can instigate activity in peers. This principle has enormously important consequences in such domains as mating behavior, the territorial organization of living space, and the maintenance of intragroup ranking—the so-called pecking order—for a great many animals, but above all for such complex and coordinated social activity as characterizes humanity and, because of this, for what we call "culture."

Culture develops through dialog distributed spatially, that is, diffused.

The spatial dynamics involved are fairly complex and only become comprehensible once dialog itself and how it produces learning are understood.

"Display in a dyad is dialog" makes a good slogan, but display includes much else besides speech. Our language seems to lack a word to cover the range of displays additional to speech that can enter into a communicative interaction between a pair of people. Let us therefore not scruple to stretch the original sense of the term "dialog," and allow it to cover exchange of all forms of display. A dialog, in either sense, consists of an exchange of utterances. The format of such exchanges has lately become an object of particular study, which has discerned some fundamental regularities in human interaction.

According to the dyadic principle, "Two's company; three's a crowd." An analysis of dialog does not work with crowds even of three, much less with larger ones. It focuses on the exclusive company of the dyad alone; the many voices in the crowd would only confound it. This evocation of a face–to–face encounter accords with the necessarily bipolar—dyadic—character of all communication, as already outlined. The model it embodies can, as will be shown, apply to encounters other than immediate, proximate ones, for instance to telephone conversations, and even to reading (as well as writing) a book, working for wages, or both sending and receiving gifts. Its essential feature is reciprocating utterance in any media between two interlocutors.

Probably, ordinary speech most clearly exemplifies the ideal format that always obtains. Hence, recently developed models of the so-called speech act have inspired the discussion that follows now.

Speech is only a part of the story. Although the format of spoken dialog affords a most welcome ideal model, all other acts of display likewise conform to it. Reflect, for example, on the striking difference between a disembodied talk on the telephone and an actual person-to-person encounter, in which facial expressions and gestures, clothing and grooming and scent, and the particular setting or "venue" with all its contents, each have bearing on what will transpire. (What good are the changing facial expressions and manual gestures of someone talking by phone?) We often express our sense of this difference by concluding our call with "Let's get together soon!" This shows how reformulation of the speech act idea to embrace the richness of direct encounter is essential for grasping the full implications, the wider consequences, of communication.

Mindful of this caution, observe now how dialog works. It is all give and take. Suppose a couple of people converse. One of them initiates the exchange with some sort of utterance, verbal or otherwise. Whatever that person says, or shows, or points out will invite a response. The opening utterance serves to designate a topic of discourse, and perhaps as well to hint at acceptable forms of reply. Thus do questions, commands, and simple assertions tend to elicit dissimilar answering displays. Each one of the pair in dialog then by turn "takes the floor," and a reciprocating sequence of utterances (always potentially involving bodily actions besides speech) carries on for a while. The duration of the exchange is at the double discretion of both parties; one partner may even decline at the start to respond, and so truncate the whole encounter. But even that eloquent abstention constitutes communication: "Silence speaks volumes."

As declared in the previous chapter, a refusal to respond to an interlocutor's challenge is rooted in freedom. As we preach to young "druggies," you can always say no—or say nothing at all. This option goes right to the heart of the speech or display act itself and also, I think, underlies and guarantees the ultimate freedom of a human being. The implications of the negative option, and of the openness of any possible responses for acts of display, derive from the nature of information in general, which has to center on novelty, on the "anti-entropic" introduction of some new degree of order into a situation.

Ordinarily, foregone conclusions are hardly worth talking about. In fact, in technical usage, the concept of information means precisely the unexpected, that which supplants or rejects the entropic, statistically most probable state of things. Remember that expression—and therefore both speech and more broadly display—seeking response always probes for information. Animals would give up the practice of emitting warning cries for their fellows if no ascertained result ever followed. A lack of survival utility would soon enough eliminate such behavior. Obviously, a clearcut question is designed to evoke a response, to scan for possible novelty, but so is any other format of utterance or, as the students of speech acts call it, any illocutionary form. These include direct questions, commands, assertions, promises, and threats, among other devices of display.

What sorts of novelty, then, may dialog disclose? Who are you? How do you feel? Where are you? Friend or foe? What can you do to me? What are you going to do? Where is it? What is this? What's going on? What must I do? Show me! People are forever asking just these kinds of questions, but of course in varied and numerous ways far beyond simply speech. And one of the commonest concerns addressed would be just "are things still all right?"—hopeful of a reassuring confirmation of the status quo: "nothing new to report" also carries useful information. Often, no news really is good news.

If one always knew in advance the answers to be expected, however, nothing new would be learned. "You might as well save your breath!" Saving one's breath indeed obeys a cornerstone natural law: nature's economy and humankind's discipline abhor the unnecessary depletion of resources, even of lungfuls of oxygen. Windbags are wasteful. An utterly idle display costs too much, and, I shall later insist, nowhere more so than where prodigal human ostentation fruitlessly squanders the bounty of nature or the patience and good will and effort of people. "Vain display" or even worse, this is the source of the most flagrant and dangerous abuses of humanity's environmental birthright.

The picture of the act of display begins now to emerge: two people taking turns at free provocations and responses, each in search of information and employing any means of utterance at hand. A good many writers have depicted or described what happens, but their emphases vary considerably. Some, for example in the speech act theories of Austin (1962) and many of his successors, construct an account that alleges a substantial traffic in specific ideas or meanings. Opting to eschew this "semantic" approach, the present more pragmatic argument draws on a different authority, that of Martin Schwab (1980), whose focus falls not on intact transfers of meaning, but on what he calls "problematization."

Schwab's valid and crucial point is that an opening elects a topic and indicates how it is to be dealt with. The response remains open and indeterminate. Not only does the conversational opener problematize something, but each ensuing turn in the dialog contributes some sort of further query, so that the dialog not only continues but also goes on switching its topic and tone bit by bit. "Don't change the subject!" a person may angrily say, but dialog always consists precisely of that!

Dialog furthermore engages the two interlocutors in an extraconversational reality affording means of authenticating what has been uttered. The illocutionary forms mentioned above firmly tie the dialog to material, real world action. This pragmatic proviso, as will be shown, renders the human transformation of the world vastly more intelligible. Put up or shut up!

Functionally, grammatical forms connect the illocutionary utterance with specific, concrete situations. They point and name and designate, and then permit illocution to formulate action. And grammar precedes illocution.

How does an interlocutor problematize something? Employing some illocutionary format constitutes only part of that operation. It commences with an indication—a deictic device—or a definition or categorization of something, a topic, which focuses on some particular of the common field of observation or imagination. Grammar prescribes what to look at or listen to, handle or sample.

A deictic reference to something, through either vocal or gestural utterance, simply indicates or points to it. Deictic devices are altogether common throughout much of the animal kingdom, and humanity's grammars employ them. Pronouns, for instance, serve a deictic function, as do also such terms as directional ones; so sometimes do nods of the head, fixed stares, and manual gestures. "Oh, look!" "Hey, you there!" or a pointing hand zero in on the subject of interest. This kind of display behavior is brilliantly and exhaustively treated in William Hanks' book (1990) on referential practice among the modern Maya.

In grammar, pronouns count as a particular "part of speech," and as noted, even gestures can fulfill a function parallel to theirs. Another grammatical part of speech, called prepositions, may serve a related, directional function. "Near" and "in" and "among" and "across" instruct about where to look.

What grammarians call nouns—referring to persons, places, or things—may also serve a directive function. They too can either nominate a topic or, we may say, "objectify" it and incorporate it with a predicate—a proposed attribute—of some sort. But whereas a bodily gesture, or even some types of exclamations, can frequently direct the attention of an interlocutor even in the absence of a common verbal language—they do pretty well even with dogs: you can whistle for Fido—the successful use of nouns usually requires a shared language as medium. And of course even a supposedly common idiom may fail to guarantee full comprehension; calling a spade a spade may not work with an ignorant partner who knows only "shovel." Physicians and lawyers are expert in learned obfuscation of that kind. "What's in a name," indeed?

Adjectives predicate. They assign a sensory characterization or some other attribute to what is observed or discussed. In so doing, they help to indicate the topic at issue, just as do nouns. Possessive adjectives and names and other nouns in particular behave deictically. All adjectival usage depends on selecting some one or a few out of the infinite possible attributes of an object, however. If we specify "a green lampshade" and let it go at that, we indicate implicitly that we may not wish at the moment to discuss also its texture, its chemical composition, its price, its age, and its shape. Furthermore, adjectives, like nouns, can be misunderstood. A good exercise in incomprehension can be had by trying to discuss subtle shades of color with a painter or a dress buyer.

Among all the conventional parts of speech, the verb is perhaps the most interesting. Again, its use can result in great misunderstanding. Yet whenever it functions successfully, a verb does a wonderful thing: it converts the highly complex and diverse buzz of sensory stimuli emanating from a given shared field of experience into a focal event. Imagine a typical scene in a kitchen: shall we talk about the fact that Joe is sitting in a chair reading (or, if illiterate, just staring at) a newspaper? or shall we call attention to the burning toast or spilled coffee? or take note of the dog feasting uninvited on the bacon and eggs? or just criticize someone's table decorum? A million and more observable features and minor events present themselves at every instant. What shall be singled out for remark? What's happening?

It might be conjectured, incidentally, that certain animal signals also accomplish a rudimentary verb function, as in the case of the cries of sentinel prairie dogs and the yelps that may coordinate the hunting tactics of wolf packs. Particular monkey vocalizations and rats' alarm squeals may similarly foreshadow the part played by verbs in a language, for they convey a focus on an event that may be threatening. Such a suggestion presages the far more versatile illocutionary use of verbs in human languages as an overwhelmingly important unique feature.

Grammars often distinguish between the verb proper and the so-called copula. The latter, rather than calling attention to an action or event, equates two nouns or pairs nouns with adjectives: $x = y$. But the true verb, more narrowly considered, depicts a notable event, process, or action. Yet it can make whatever it indicates subject to almost any sort of characterization. Verbs expressly betoken a situation's significance for possible action, in a way that deictics for instance do not. Their great utility resides in the fact that events or situations they pinpoint often evoke an active response that makes use of objects.

The part played by objects in the verb-construed action world of humanity has decisive bearing on the manner in which the species is able to modify that world so effectively. Hence the important role of objects not only in action, but particularly in that part of it consisting explicitly of communication, must next be considered.

FOUR

• Show and Tell

When someone mutters, "Stick 'em up!" it's nice to be sure they mean "Hang up the posters," not something more threatening.

Prudent people suddenly modify their behavior when they notice that the stranger facing them has a gun. Mere material objects and even evanescent gestures frequently serve as powerful means of expression. In effect we endow them with "voices" of their own, comparable and complementary to oral speech itself. In this manner, objects often generate Geltung.

At the outset, let us understand that communication consists purely of actions—and actions alone—and never of objects as such, although human actions alluding to objects—invoking them, giving them voices—form a decidedly important part of communication.

The human repertory of communicative actions goes well beyond speaking as such, obviously taking in gestures as well, for example. In this regard, the concept of display again proves heuristic, because it lends a special emphasis to the act (either linguistic or gestural) of showing things to interlocutors—literally, to displaying objects before them. That kind of action constitutes a crucial part of human dialog and contributes much, as I shall continue to show, to human agency in nature.

Do elephants never forget? People do. But they have ways of recalling through discourse and artifacts. The human individual's capacity to learn lifelong from peers of course includes the ability to profit from witnessing object displays, and as will become evident, the stable and enduring form of the latter can markedly enhance cultural continuity by, as it were, "fossilizing" gestures. Just consider how the Koran and Sutras and Bible continue to influence action. That is, enduring eloquent objects permit transcendence of time; Ozymandias did not have it completely wrong!

"Let sleeping dogs lie" wouldn't make sense if no one had ever got bit for disturbing an ill-tempered cur. What we say in so many words, or otherwise proclaim in the abstract, craves concrete examples or proofs. The various illocutionary forms and grammatical (or even "ungrammatical") parts of speech distinguished by students of speech acts each presume their own proper verification procedures. For example, we compliment people when we say they're "as good as their word," implying that they keep their promises, for an unfulfilled promise is really no promise at all. Similarly, in order to accept an ostensibly factual assertion, we may demand a concrete confirmation; seeing is believing. Again, a command disobeyed is no command at all, but something more like a reproach to its utterer. Notice that here it takes two participants to confirm or reject the command. Even a mere exclamation may invite testing; when someone says "ouch!" we ask, "Where does it hurt?" A crybaby quickly loses credibility.

We go so far, in fact, as to doubt even questions; thus, a bossy inquiry may spur the response, "Are you asking me or telling me?" Or one can query coyly, "Do you really want to know?" And a threat is often dissolved by "I dare you!" Allegations, questions, promises, advice, threats, complaints, demands, accusations, orders, exclamations, and perhaps as many more illocutionary categories as one chooses to distinguish, all connote a situation in which a speech act or display depends for its validity upon at least the possibility of an independent, real world demonstration of some kind. False praise becomes damaging flattery. Talking big booby-traps a boaster.

The children's game of "Show and Tell" actually imitates the normal flow of all human dialog, which almost invariably consists not only of reciprocating utterances by two partners, but furthermore of the continual interweaving of various kinds of expressive media. We do keep on showing as we tell and telling while we show. Sometimes the nonvocal element is so prominent that, perhaps, we may be able to deduce the gist of a conversation just by observing the gestures from a distance, or watching something change hands. For human communication, even the heavens help out: notice how useful the moon can be to romance!

In the course of our constant probing for new information, we need to get outside the strict bounds of dialog and deal with an object world.

In doing so, we may grossly alter that world. The very activities required to substantiate a statement or undertaking, for example, themselves constitute acts of display, some of which may perceptibly affect the habitat. Just as answering a question, for example, involves showing or saying something, conformity with an order is signaled by an observable activity that may change the inanimate surroundings. So again, when display begets further display it may have enduring physical consequences.

What sorts of displays can one individual exhibit to another in order to stimulate or sustain interaction, in other words as a provocation to communicate? We can utter—express or give forth—much besides words. An exceedingly wide and diverse range of media presents itself, beginning with speech and other vocalizations that consist of coordinated gestural use of many organs from the diaphragm to the tongue and lips, then extending to additional bodily gestures employing the numerous delicate facial muscles, the limbs, or the general posture. In addition, any adornment or modification of the parts of the body surface itself, such as its painting, dyeing, dressing, or tattooing, help to shape the context of communication and under certain circumstances execute its major functions. "Dress for success" is not bad advice.

Besides the foregoing list of bodily adornments, a potentially unlimited variety of further artifactual accessories and even simple natural objects may play major roles as media of communication.

Do "actions speak louder than words"? Yes, probably so, according to the reasoning just advanced above. At the very least, actions make words more convincing. "Don't do as I say; do as I do." It is fair to assume, then, that physical, bodily actions additional to those involved in producing speech must also constitute important media of display, and therefore of communication. Particular postures and gestures, including those involved in performing physical work, are included among them. Does not this criterion perhaps qualify human labor itself as communicative activity? Work reveals the real person.

Yet another common phrase may provide some illumination: confronting a nonobjective painting, hearing a cryptic rumor, or discovering a dollar in our shoe, we ask, "What do you make of it?" This question hints that objects, or for that matter events and actions (singled out for remark by a verb!), can take on whatever communicative function we care to assign to them. Then a person can make any object or episode, representational or not, count and signify as display. We can conceivably make just about anything, even natural objects that run a gamut from grains of sand to storms and sunsets and subatomic particles, carry a "message" or, better, provocative power. All of them "speak"—when invoked and attended to, but not otherwise.

This principle of free interchangeability among any and all types of display media (cf. "He said he was sorry; she merely nodded and gave back the ring") accounts for the overwhelming importance of human communication per se for environmental modification. Acknowledgment of the principle of interchangeability of media allows a reassessment of two highly central and familiar features of human activity, the trading of goods and services for money, compensation in kind, or other considerations and one individual's performance of work for another, again in exchange for some compensation. Both those related forms of human activity are crucial in altering environments. And we postulate securely that the use of all such devices expediting dialog must obey at least one primitive motive: to get a response.

Genuine communication, including labor and commerce, should, as modern technical devices illustrate, provide not only a means of sending messages but one for receiving them too. It should compose a closed circuit, so that reciprocating dialog can proceed. In consequence, the ostensibly complete action or unitary instrument may well count for something only when linked into a multimembered system, perhaps comprised of very dissimilar components.

Because they provide communicators with a surrogate situation for the normal face-to-face encounter, all technical means or carriers must expectably modify acts of display in various ways. Yet the only rationale for using them lies in "getting one's message across"—and also, remember, thereby seeking response. Circuitry serves to connect the senders and receivers.

Probably the most poignant instance of a technical device designed for this purpose is the vehicle the Americans consigned to outer space in order to portray our world to whatever extraterrestrial beings might chance upon it. Will the human figures and other engravings on its golden surface ever be seen by unearthly eyes (or similar organs)? What will they possibly "mean" to creatures in the distant cosmos?

Should we scoff at the naïveté of the project? Not so, I maintain: forget about meaning and only recall that, according to the principles elucidated in this chapter, they may elicit responses. Exactly because the designs may look cryptic to inhabitants of planets in some distant galaxy, the inscriptions may incite the strangers to investigate our world and thus perhaps reveal themselves to us.

Many less audacious feats of engineering, as well as humbler artifactual developments that have long existed, extend the temporal and also spatial range of dialog on earth between a pair of interlocutors. The multiplicity of means of this sort has latterly become spectacular. Our vocabularies lacked such terms as FAX and video, camcorder and cellular phone, and laptop computer only a decade or so ago. In general, however, such recent artifacts merely accelerate, intensify, refine, or enhance in some other way the functions performed by earlier technical means. Furthermore, any conceivable technical devices serving communication must in principle exhibit certain common properties, and the message traffic over them must still conform to all the stipulations introduced so far in this discussion.

Television broadcasts seem to offer prime examples of true "mass" communication. It appears as if their messages are simply scattered on the wind. But the idea of real one-way mass communication contradicts the dyad principle and has to be refuted. Consider a typical television program, say a "soap opera." The actors address their lines and exhibit their antics to an audience, but does the audience address them back? Of course it does! The watchers either purchase the product or, if nobody buys their brand of soap, the actors go off the air. That is the merciless law of the TV jungle and also of other such so-called mass media. The circuits close, often with deadly, strangling effect.

Communication must be both give and take. And it also seeks new information: in the present TV example, some of the audience looks for new hairdos and others lie in wait for reusable wisecracks, whereas the actors and all the establishment backing them up literally try to see how much money they can make. It should be remarked that, in this exemplary case, extremely diverse components will make up the total circuit between a given member of the audience and the actors; the many steps involved can be left to the reader's imagination.

Among the most telling displays that we seek and heed are exactly those among objects and actions affecting them. This is the reason that the particular circuits of communication established in labor and trade, whether or not configured through artifacts, exert overwhelming effects in modifying material environments and hence human living conditions. The fictions attached to those odd little objects called money can and do make the world over.

"There are things that money can't buy," to be sure. But we need to consider precisely some things that money plainly can buy. The dyadic process of human display avails itself of the interchangeability of speech, gestures, and objects, including paychecks and cash, invoked as utterance, in order to manage not only the transfer of money and services and goods among people but also the exchange of effort and time against rewarding responses.

Contemplating dialog in the fashion proposed makes it easy to understand the communicative or, more specifically, the display value of all sorts of objects. Manipulation and modification of various items of environmental content often take place in the course of display. Such effects may arise as no more than inadvertent or irrelevant by-products of the gestures produced, and indeed even the latter may occur independently enough of the main display as possibly to contradict it—as when, for example, a cringing posture negates brave assertions. In fact, the way in which objects, and actually even certain gestures, enter significantly into communicative interaction—that is, the method of using them— has more importance than the particular character of the given things or movements themselves. Remember that the effective involvement of objects in a display only takes place through explicit allusion to them in one form or another; their presence otherwise, even as part of the context, means little.

The present argument, holding that it is above all its elaborated system of communication, and of course the permanent practice of imitative learning that underlies it, that sets humanity apart, takes issue with many prevalent interpretations, including in particular the highly influential opinions of Marx. Regarding the collaboration of individuals in society as primarily directed to securing a collective livelihood, he considered the habit of productive labor to be what most markedly distinguishes humanity from all other creatures. Other features of human behavior and culture—the social divison of labor and system of classes and their "superstructure"—he construed as outgrowths or consequences of the productive base system.

Does the model proposed for acts of display not lend a more functional sense to the commodity value idea introduced by Karl Marx? Under this Marxian formulation, material production dominates social relationships, and control or ownership of the instruments used for it also implies control of labor time and therefore of wealth. In the sphere of trade and commerce, the "fetishism of commodities" promotes exchange practices under which articles circulate not in response to their use value—their inherent worth as means of keeping alive (reproducing) a society—but in obedience instead to attributed commodity value, that is, usefulness as mere showpieces or tokens accumulated and used in exchange, such as money itself. The triumph of commodity value over use value opens the gates to grossly uneven amassing of wealth among individuals. This Marxian emphasis on commodity value itself would attest to the primacy of communicative over "practical," utilitarian determinants of human activity.

We might accept the essence of the Marxian interpretation but, following a trend of thought developed by Marshall Sahlins (1976), Mary Douglas and Baron Isherwood (1979), and Jean Baudrillard (1968, 1972), consider not concrete material production but the communication that manages both it and much else besides, as primary, and the control of the means of communication, including the prestige to which "commodity fetishism" alludes, as the key to control of production, exchange, and accumulation and the source of societal dominance. By far the most crucial means of production, in other words, are those producing communication itself, that is, generating, managing, and disseminating the interindividual provocations or stimuli herein termed displays, which incite all further displays, including those involved in practical work.

Here, commodity value comes first. Jean Baudrillard's analysis, for instance, contemplates communication in the perspective of what he calls "the political economy of the sign." It concerns the propensity of an economy to generate "sign" or semantic value through, or in addition to, the production of goods in the common sense. Apart from its appeal to semiotics, which is quite alien to the spirit of this essay, the pertinence of Baudrillard's notion lies in its denial of the long-prevalent utilitarian doctrine, which has emphasized security of livelihood as the sole goal of production and awarded precedence to the calculus of value in such terms.

The labor theory of value propounded by Marx seems accordingly to miss the point. Such transactions as those between work and wage payment do not rely on either the obvious importance of human effort and time in production or livelihood utility inhering in what is produced. Instead they depend on a currency of what Baudrillard calls signs and I call just provocations, within which considerations of prestige count far more heavily than such mere ostensible practicalities.

The commodity (or "sign") value in evidence here is the fundamental basis not only of labor and its recompense but clearly also of all material exchange. And this is nowhere better illustrated than in the case of money.

"Money talks" makes very good sense. A coin or a paper bill says right on its face how much it is worth. But in a much broader, illocutionary sense, one can conceive of such tokens, or even of abstractions of their values, as promises. Look at an American banknote: it engages the government in so many words to "pay to the bearer on demand." Furthermore, like Canadian bills, it is labeled as "legal tender," which signifies that it must be accepted in trade or the payment of debts.

Correspondingly, a business will post a price on each article it offers for sale, and the charge for admission to a concert or movie is prominently displayed on the premises. These are instances of money talking, and what they are saying tells something momentous. The example of the concert hall or theater puts it squarely: paying admission is just another one of those everyday rites of passage to be further discussed in a subsequent chapter.

The case of buying something in a shop may seem rather more complicated, understandably so, because it involves not merely crossing a boundary but also performing a provocative act. Just try to walk out of a store carrying an article you haven't paid for, and you'll get the point— if not arrested! As Chapter 8 details, rites of passage usually do involve much more than just progressions through space; whether in elaborate religious or military ceremonies, or in customer behavior, they tend to include special performances adjusted to the particular stage and station in the venue or scene of the action. "Now you may kiss the bride" is akin to "Shall I wrap it for you?"

If giving gifts and receiving them can communicate something, why should not selling and buying? Everything bought and sold, traded, paid, or acknowledged as owed acts in illocutionary fashion as a promissory token in communicative interaction. You are promising to the sales clerk or the company, "Here, you may go buy something with this money," and the reply is, "You may keep what you're carrying out." These exchanges call for a suitable common medium (of display), and money works very well; it does talk. The Geltung attaching to money is plain.

Certain bits of ethnographic evidence in fact intimate that, even before some troublemaker had invented money and perhaps even before it was safe and comfortable to meet in person and swap things, people engaged in a primitive kind of "silent exchange," merely dumping the things to be traded in a remote spot, where each transactor came alone and in stealth to pick up the respective proffered objects. Another very ancient form of exchange, rather unpleasant, corresponds to the phrase "Winner take all." Winners and conquerors in the past, and even more recently, have indeed not shown themselves reluctant to help themselves to whatever property of the vanquished they liked. Thus an acquired status that confers fearsomely obvious Geltung can serve as a token at least as readily as money can; take note of the guy with the gun! Nowadays, in conditions sporadically closer to peace, equality, and easy direct interaction, some people may prefer to propitiate or indemnify those from whom they take things, that is, to pay up.

Notice too that, conforming to principles stated above, either object tokens or action tokens circulate freely in exchange, which is why we lump goods and services together. A rock concert or a spirit medium's predictions enter just as readily into trade as do diamond rings and dishwasher soap. Any medium whatever may serve in commodity exchange, as in any other communicative activity. A person's labor can be bought and sold just as easily as anything else. Hours for sale!

In accordance with principles developed in previous paragraphs, we can interpret work as communicative activity for at least two reasons. First, as either verbal or gestural bodily utterance, it constitutes a valid medium of display. Second, it manifestly often or always enters somehow into the ritual of exchange described just above. Even the lofty labor of the physician costs money, after all. To be sure, we dignify the doctors' doings by paying "fees" for them, whereas a director receives an "honorarium," an executive a "salary," a professor a "stipend," and a worker merely a "wage." The system drips with discriminatory ceremoniality. This again indicates that remunerative work or even the reluctant obedience of docile slaves communicates something and fits into a formalized, cryptically ceremonial interactive performance.

Another curious fact reinforces the foregoing conclusion: the notorious tendency of the secure and privileged to continue to work, after a fashion, even once they have accumulated vast fortunes and estates. They may simply go on to increase their wealth by continuing business or else exert themselves equally hard in some other pursuit having equally little to do with mere bodily survival (except perhaps to imperil it, as in auto racing and polo).

The preceding argument need not by any means gainsay the relevance of labor to livelihood. As we all know, however, a sharp disproportion obtains between the amount of labor expended, whether measured in kilojoules or by a time clock, and the returns to the worker's livelihood. Almost everywhere, throughout history, those who have labored the least in a simple physical sense have acquired the most and the best of the goods of this world. The supposed alterations in the "relations of production" introduced by socialism have not changed this condition by much.

This typical disparity between total input of work and output of benefits makes it reasonable to suggest that the manifest, purely physical, sweaty, gross muscular contributions of an individual to the production of livelihood utilities seldom correlate closely with that individual's share of the proceeds of his or her own and all others' efforts. Something else than physical toil determines rewards.

In the ugly instance even of slavery, something is gained by victims of the systems who obey, namely survival. Compliance communicates propitiation. In contrast, the threat of serious violence hangs over the slave who does not comply with commands. Only the most courageous rebel in defense of their self-determination and dignity, frequently paying a terrible cost. Those mostly anonymous, desperate heroes have stood fast for the freedom enshrined in unique human dialog. Even labor coerced, like labor in general, obeys a dialog format.

The foregoing considerations themselves invite the conclusion that an "economy of symbols" must, as Baudrillard proposes, lie behind and dominate the ostensibly utilitarian order of production and exchange. What matters here is not the particular symbolism involved, however, but the mechanisms that create and disseminate them, that is, communicative displays.

The so-called economy of symbols, which I might prefer to call a Geltung market, equally deserves to be envisioned as an extended system of production and consumption, a spatial economy. Generated by communication, it functions through ongoing communicative activity over highly developed and distinctive spatial and temporal structures and itself perpetually works to structure and restructure environments. Geltung plays a decisive part in its operation. Therefore, its character can only be understood once the nature and effects of human Geltung itself, and the spatial influence exerted by it, are more fully described. The next chapter deals with the sources of Geltung.

FIVE

• Proverbial Geltung

The dashing General Patton was tough, brooking no hint of disrespect. Once, inspecting his troops in the field, they say, he had his jeep stop to query a Signal Corps soldier just down from a perch on a telephone pole.

The soldier slouched up to the general, neither duly reporting nor even saluting. George Patton was outraged.

"Soldier, don't you know who I am?" he roared.

"Oh, yes," acknowledged the private first class, as he clambered quickly into his vehicle. "Do you know who I am, sir?"

And with that, he sped hastily away.

Much of an individual's fate depends on recognition of identity by others. People oftener strive to proclaim, if not truly reveal, an identity than they try to conceal one entirely. Yet exaggeration and pretension tend to tinge the personal presentations of all but the few entirely candid, most modest of people. Not many care to emulate Montaigne and Rousseau in trying to tell all. (Am I seeking for Geltung by such name-dropping?)

Humanity has to appraise individuals according to the masks they affect and their essence contrived for public display, trusting to shrewdness and skepticism to counteract gullibility. A few particular aspects of people's appearance, behavior, condition, and reputation have long attracted the most attention and appraisal. These constitute tokens of Geltung.

Only rarely does a single episode of dialog result in total reproof and general public odium, or absolute approbation and widespread popularity, for either party to the exchange. Usually, people insist on announcing, in either depreciation or extenuation, that "nobody's all that good, and nobody's all that bad." Few occasions arise for an individual to capture a cynosure moment and exploit it as a single definitive declaration that harvests either glory or opprobrium. The paltry platforms of everyday life upon which we stand to display our pretensions do not entertain the wider world's interest, or awaken its concern. Even so, each trivial discredit or defeat a person endures tends to cast down, and every small apparent success exalts just a little. The gains and losses ordinarily exert only limited public effects. But pity the publicized personality, whose every blunder and slip the mass will devour with cannibal delight.

Commonly, reputations feed from slow diffusions, all the while that much more humdrum preoccupations intrude insistently and constantly into everyone's life. And hence the usual outcome of an interchange affects no more than immediate matters and the interlocutors alone. That is not to call those incidents unimportant, however. Predominating hugely in everyone's daily life and guiding its intimate course, "it's the little things that count." Even great persons depend on some simple dialog for courting their lovers, getting their dinner cooked, buying their shoes, and finding the bathroom.

Which currency does everyday display deem valid as its legal tender? Surely physical bearing, words pronounced, and objects exhibited, no? The foregoing chapters have said as much. But be wary, because the media traded in the mundane market of displays (duly including the familiar forms of markets for films and foods and finance!) possess their own special character, and the rates of exchange that apply reflect particular standards of their own. Imitative diffusion distributes, as personal customs and cultural elements, the standards determining personal Geltung.

It would take a pretty shrewd monkey or Martian, perhaps, to recognize that the pieces of paper that people hand round when they shop must exhibit certain physical attributes to count for anything. But a clerk alert enough can often spot the cleverest counterfeit bill. Material tokens exchanged in dyadic display must conform to exacting specifications. They have to assert their identity clearly enough to escape confusion, and although their authenticity, like that of cash, can be feigned, that assumes risks. Similarly, speech and demeanor and personal appearance have to conform to standards of their own and have to seem sincere and genuine in order to merit credit, although these attributes too support whole industries of falsification.

Life would turn out sadly bland if that were all that we looked for in displays, however. Their effectiveness rests on a minor quotum of novelty. New information, in digestible servings, is always the currency. Variety is not simply the spice of life, it also has to lend flavor to every display. The little bit of piquancy creates the appetite for fare to nourish communication.

Be careful, though, not to season the mixture too richly, lest it lose its palatability. A little will go a long way! The display you serve up must modestly conform as well as beguile. Officious old Polonius was right: ". . . nor any unproportioned thought his act." That venerable lord Chamberlain seems to have possessed an expert's understanding of Geltung, although too full of himself. Probably people who dwell too much on their Geltung do strike others the same way. So it helps to play it cool. The odds on an aleatory bid for Geltung go against the players who tip their cards too incautiously. Respect rewards reserve.

Social psychologists frequently test and chart and compare the effects of various "presentations of self" on observers and have produced an extensive literature on the subject. A probably equally large amount of popularizing comment and counsel constantly issues from the everyday press. Then, too, private conversations filled with facile assessments of people not present are extremely commonplace. Such intense concentration on crucial "superficialities" does not occur accidentally. Nature made us notice and care.

Like many other animals, every normal member of the human species is apparently natively programmed and well equipped to pay almost compulsory attention to any peer's activity. The highly differentiated facial and manual musculature and the functional capacities of the brain and sensory organs themselves reflect this predisposition. The capacity to recognize a particular human countenance has developed astoundingly far beyond the ability to distinguish other objects in the environment. Furthermore, the eye can pick up the subtlest modulations of expression in the labile tensions of the face, in particular, and also only slightly less adeptly, in a somewhat subliminal fashion, any fine but telling readjustment of bodily posture. Likewise the human ear detects almost infinitesimal features of vocalization, such as pitch and stress and duration and cadence, among the strictures and resonances in the vocal apparatus that transform the breath into speech. These properties show conclusively how our focus is fixed on our fellows.

What signs do people consult, then, in evaluating others so keenly and arriving at readiness to respond to them? What triggers their counterdisplays?

Any shrewd merchant, any courtroom lawyer, any talented novelist knows some of the answers to those questions. But so do ordinary people, although perhaps unskilled in expressing them. But lore accumulated over centuries distils and preserves the time-tested insights of countless anonymous observers, unceasingly refreshed and winnowed out by each generation. Maxims and proverbs in every language retail them.

An old Dutch saying pronounces that "proverbs are the daughters of daily experience." As if to caution against too much trust in them, however, another old saying warns that "wise men make proverbs and fools repeat them." I shall nevertheless take the plunge and call on some proverbs to implement my discussion. A somewhat craven device makes this possible. To wit, I consulted a well-known dictionary of American and European proverbs in gathering my ammunition. Please excuse the plagiarism!

What sorts of precepts purportedly foretell what a person will be like? Here is a sample snippet from the sixteenth century that says a good deal about how people look upon outward appearance:

Fair and foolish,
Little and loud,
Long and lazy,
Black and proud;
Fat and merry,
Lean and sad,
Pale and peevish,
Red [hair? dress?] and bad.

Maybe gentlemen do prefer blondes, but the image of the "dumb blonde" echoes this much older doggerel. The quotation anticipates the "little Napoleon" figure, as well, and some other prejudgments still among us. Falstaff appears in it, along with Othello, Werther perhaps, and Scrooge himself. It attests to the durability of popular bases of appraisal and recalls their embodiments in literature.

Proverbs provide a number of not very philanthropic rules for observing and judging one's neighbor. They seem however to summarize fairly the practice of typical people today or whenever. Two kinds of criteria stand out: the appearance alone and the reputation, the one impression direct and the other diffused.

What kinds of appearances count?

"For the Lord seeth not as man seeth; for man looketh on the outward appearance, but the Lord looketh on the heart" (1 Sam. 16:7). Given that truth from the Bible, caution and canniness profit. "Foretold is forewarned," as somebody said; and a Latin proverb goes on, "Forewarned, forearmed." That paranoid-sounding advice applies, of course, as much to deciding what to wear to a party, or whether a guest will eat kidney pie, as to darker forebodings. Assessment of people need not only be fearful, thank goodness!

Long observation gave rise to certain generalities that aid the interpretation of behavior. One proverb touches on the advantages of conformity and ordinariness: "Do as most men do, and men will speak well of you."

Such an injunction succinctly captures the concept of culture. But its relevance certainly extends no further than the bounds of the given country or community in which an individual lives. People behaving in the customary ways of their homelands often find themselves confronted with incredulity or worse when they sojourn in a strange land. They are then likely to dismiss the indigenous culture as uncouth or inhumane. Ever since the great age of Greece, the term "barbarian" has settled on anything unfamiliar or alien. Nevertheless, the advice the maxim provides does not err by much, for stay-at-homes, at least. And it nicely predicts how most of us meekly adapt, most of the time.

Unfortunately or otherwise, though, no total uniformity prevails in any known culture. People differ in habit according to station and upbringing. No perfect consensus ever exists. Then with whom should an individual seek to identify? Only immediate circumstance tells, and that reflects the momentary venue and its pertinent tradition, along with whatever standards circulate among the wider community. No wonder, as yet another proverb puts it, "He must rise early that would please everybody."

"There would be no great ones if there were no little ones," one proverb tells us. Disparity and difference among a population impose yet other refinements. In spite of mutual dependence, jealously cherished dissimilarities mark the demeanor of individuals of varied social position, exacting either grudging deference or haughty depreciation. "The great would have none great, and the little all little."

But eminence calls for great care and circumspection: "He sits not sure that sits too high." For sadly, in this cold, cruel world, a proverb says it aright: "He that is down, down with him." The saying "He that thinks too much of his virtues bids others to think of his vices" rings true. And noblesse oblige—rank imposes obligations. "He that is a master must serve." Only "he that is master of himself will soon be master of others."

Some occasions submit an individual to full assessment better than others do. Constant close association opens the eyes of companions, even if familiarity need not always breed contempt. People in public positions have to reckon with augmented exposure to critical attention and evaluation all the time. Everyone, however, has to face some amount of the same.

"In sports and journeys men are known" strikes home. Having published some research on amateur sport (Wagner, 1981), I can vouch for the intimate connection between personal Geltung and sporting performance. Athletes dress their bodies for the game and undress their souls for the crowd. Contenders learn in the contest to know either their innermost selves or some delectable simulacrum of them confected by publicity. The champions feast on the frenzy of partisan fans. Records broken are reputations made.

As for journeys, anyone who ever suffered through a long, painful trip with a previously unsuspected sluggard, boor, or ignoramus acquaintance or camped with a slatternly, selfish companion will appreciate the aptness of the proverb.

The cultural and circumstantial aspects hastily summarized above do not exhaust the subject of criteria germane to judgments of displays, nor the store of proverbs pertaining to them. Here are more.

Bodily conformation counts in encounter. Imposing physical stature, even sometimes a touch of portliness, makes a decided impression. Charlemagne and Peter the Great and Fidel Castro have loomed as comparative giants in more ways than one. And American presidents tend to come tall.

Psychological testing has shown, in fact, that respondents, in America at least, overestimate the height of prominent persons. Even when we say "a great woman" or "a big man in politics," we unwittingly enlarge the physical person. Size and respect are connected.

Corpulent persons hardly can fail to make a correspondingly weighty impression. The late queen of Tahiti grew to enormous, much admired dimensions. The Spanish conquistadors met a doughty foe in southern Mexico, the warlike Chiapanecs, led into battle by an imposing, grossly fat female, whom they subsequently hacked to scraps in the fray. In the Arabic countries of North Africa, and also Uganda, the powerful men allegedly prefer to collect obese wives.

Notoriously, too, comeliness commends to admiration and acceptance, if not always also to respect. Somehow "the beautiful people" had to be the lucky, successful, carefree ones deserving of envy and emulation. Whatever personal beauty may be—and the standards vary around the world—it registers as telling display and earns its quota of positive Geltung. What the Western world accepts as entertainment has to feature fetching forms and faces. "Beauty is only skin deep," but, oh! what a lovely skin.

In vain do the proverbs admonish us that "beauty without bounty avails not" and "beauty is potent, but money is omnipotent." Nor, overlooking examples like Samson's Delilah and Becky Sharp, do we like to regard good looks as possibly treacherous.

Often, a deceptively "honest face" in a stranger brings someone's judgment and checkbook to grief. And men who "can't resist a pretty face" fall prey to disappointments. A handsome visage and wavy greying hair to set it off have helped elect people like President Warren Gamaliel Harding and other dismal nonentities. Politics prefers a pretty portrait.

Proverbially again, "A good face is a letter of recommendation." The term "face" in common usage now may derive from corresponding terms in Oriental languages, such as *menmoku* ("face—eye") in Japanese, from Chinese roots. It refers, obviously, to more than corporeal features yet suggests that those literally belong in the forefront. Losing face or gaining it are exemplary Geltung phenomena. Facing down someone is a put-down, too.

Having had hippies introduce a previous section, I have to make mention of hair. You might well have supposed that the aversion to youthful long locks originated with the crabby critics of the movement of the sixties. But here is a proverb to contest that notion: "More hair than wit," which stems from the sixteenth century. In the century following that one, the Roundheads of Cromwell made a point of cropping their tresses to distance themselves from the curly-maned nobles supporting the poor doomed King Charles. Never imagine that hair doesn't matter; now still it obsesses a great many daughters and sons.

Shakespeare made Polonius pronounce that "the apparel oft proclaims the man." When I stroll around Vancouver, I can spot the young executives in business suits, with seemly curls crawling down to their collars; servile clerks in shirtsleeves in summer, choking on obligate neckties; impeccable secretaries wearing most of their salary to work. Their clothes not only enhance their appearance but also aim to accredit them all to some particular audience. A proverb has put it, "Good clothes open all doors," but more specific standards of dress likewise exist for all sorts of very special doors.

Costume contrasting with their daytime dress admits the same people to recreations of the night. Vancouverites may dress at dawn to go jogging, after work again for the ski slopes or tennis, and yet again before dining in town. Gardening garb, travel togs, and Sunday lounging robe and slippers all expand the inventory. More than one person lives in that clothes closet.

A solid citizen can comfortably quote another proverb: "In my own city my name, in a strange city my clothes procure me respect." This principle need not imply uniformity, however. Exotic costumes, unlike most alien cultural features, seem throughout history to have enhanced the prospects of ambassadors to foreign courts. Arab delegates make an impression when they sweep through the halls of the United Nations in capacious long robes and burnooses.

As just illustrated, a good deal more than vague respect is involved. Raiment claims attention and classifies persons. Conforming to the dyadic principle, the declaration clothing delivers, like that of any other display, addresses itself to specific people in selected places and often alludes to hierarchical status within those milieus. A clerkish tie will always mark the manager in supermarkets, and a modest smock will signify a checker. Watching trials in Canadian courtrooms is more fun than in American ones, because the judges appear in grandiose gowns and ridiculous wigs, and the lawyers have to drape themselves in black and dangle stringy white ties from their throats.

My collection of proverbs proves culture bound. The Western preoccupations with both youth and utility utterly color them. Were I to look among the maxims of Oriental countries, I surely would find an entirely dissimilar view expressed about age, although not about women, no doubt. The elders of many societies have always enjoyed great respect, and their words were well heeded, but here in our countries we incline to shelve them away in retirement oblivion, understandingly saying little about it.

Rather unexpectedly, it is Henry David Thoreau who best sums up the prevalent youthful, insolent North American view in his *Walden*: "I have lived some thirty years on this planet and I have yet to hear the first syllable of valuable or even earnest advice from my seniors."

Only a few of the proverbs I find have anything much to say about old people. One stingily concedes, as if it were news, that "old age is honourable," and another admits that "old age, though despised, is coveted by all"—purely, no doubt, in preference to early death.

A few sayings mention generational conflict: "Youth and age will never agree" and "Young men think old men fools, and old men know young men to be so." The old French saying, "*Si jeunesse savait, si vieillesse pouvait!*" (If youth but knew, if age but could!), expresses little more than envy. And people who say "Age before beauty" at the door like to turn it into a joke.

Hierarchical seniority, along with the income it brings, rather than age, appears to impress the West most. Perquisites flow from position. Learning and wisdom garner more Geltung in other societies. One proverb does allow stingily that "knowledge is no burden," and the favorite of all betrays a Western preoccupation again: "Knowledge is power." An even more revealing one says that "knowledge makes one laugh [*sic*], but wealth makes one dance"; it sounds like a teenager's precept.

The German sociologist Ferdinand Tönnies drew an illuminating distinction between the spontaneous "Gemeinschaft" or primary community, and the secondary, task-oriented "Gesellschaft" or society, propelled by the principles of collective rationality. The former, more ancient and traditional kind of human organization exhibits a fairly amorphous spatial character, a set of highly localized village constellations tied into few extensive networks, whereas a modern, innovative social system, invariably urbanized, shows an abundance of complex interlacing connections and sharply discrete domains. The difference declares itself in the standards of recognized virtue and merit: Age receives honor in villages; youth does in cities.

"A man is as old as he feels," claims one proverb, "and a woman as old as she looks." Youth again emphasized! The proverbs I have access to without exception disparage women in general, yet many exalt individual female beauty and true love. "Women are necessary evils," asserts one ungracious sixteenth-century proverb. (I decline to cite any more of this kind; their tone dismays and annoys me.) Unmistakable misogyny exudes from the mass of popular adages. Their cynical incomprehension smacks of veiled fear. The unknown "dead white males" who coined and diffused the proverbs we recite apparently have always heretofore extolled only women's physical charms and subservience. On the evidence, it is hard to deny that a feminist movement was long overdue.

At present, women aware of their ancient Geltung disadvantage increasingly gravitate toward activism and the public life. More elderly folk will have forfeited even those chances through irreparable delay. The proverbs of Europe and America indicate that whatever efforts individuals make, the criteria covering words and deeds continue expressing a bias toward youthful, masculine virtues nevertheless.

But static appearance alone does not mean everything. Now consider how manifest actions and objects also discriminate personal Geltung.

SIX

• Actions Speak Louder

One constant admonition runs through all counsel, ancient and modern, bearing on speech. "More have repented speech than silence"; "Speak fitly or be silent wise"; "Speak fair and think what you will." Such themes stand forth in fables and biblical books as clearly as in modern manuals of self-improvement. The laconic man of few words is admired; such a woman may almost be feared. "Bare words make no bargain," for "Great talkers are great liars." Proverbially, too, "He that once deceives is ever suspected"; "He that promises too much means nothing"; "Truth needs not many words."

As if to compensate for the falsity permitted only to people by speech, that other unique human attribute, humor, lightens the load of a dialog and disarmingly gets around tensions. Upon the introduction of an altogether unexpected climax to a tale—a legitimate but startling conclusion drawn from a set of premises—often interlocutors drop their guard. Jokes jostle defenses.

Loquaciousness, in many cultures, does have its place. President Castro did not himself invent long-winded speeches; his precedents go back to the sachems of the Iroquois Confederation, East African chiefs, and famous congressional orators, such as Daniel Webster and William Jennings Bryan. But often, speaking is a privilege of rank. Silence becomes the more humble.

The maxim that "Actions speak louder than words" would seem obvious enough. Speaking more than botanically, "Deeds are fruits, words are but leaves," and "A man of words and not of deeds is like a garden full of weeds."

Such injunctions seem to commend a style of communication taking advantage of the multiplicity of media additional to speech and tend to suggest a significant rule: that however interchangeable they be, speech and gesture and demonstrations of various sorts can carry unequal effect in expressing the same given impulse. Recall illocution!

Action brings perils for reputation with it, however. Cautious proverbs warn that "He that respects not is not respected"; "Courtesy on one side only lasts not long"; "He that hath done ill once will do it again"; "He loses his thanks who promises and delays." Why only "he"? Is it not also true of the female?

A warlike past shows through in what many proverbs assert. Courage figures as a touchstone of laudable action in particular. "Fortune favors the brave"; "The more danger, the more honour." Dryden's comment that "None but the brave deserve the fair" appears at times to hold true. But still, as a proverb shrewdly asserts, "Many would be cowards if they had courage enough," and another deflating one declares that "The more wit the less courage."

In all, we also do well to assume that "He that desires honor is not worthy of honor." "Honors change manners," and sometimes dishonorably. "Praise makes good men better and bad men worse"—and certainly women as well.

Many of the proverbs cited above would make sense in any society, but some betray a parochial view. Remember that the voice of the West does not always speak for all of humanity. Proverbs from the Bible, hortatory stories of Aesop, monitory West African tales about animals, and the classical Russian fables of Krylov, all convey their own characteristic cultural flavor, sometimes strikingly contrasting with that of the proverbs known in the West. A canvass of encapsulated prejudice and wisdom from around the world would far transcend the bounds of this present discussion, however.

One always relevant factor in action is captured in various sayings commending an apparently universal sense of place and instinct for just the proper moment to act. An exquisite etiquette governs the venues elected for proper display. Yet even Shakespeare did not go far enough: not all the world's a stage, but a million stages and more, each with its own dramatis personae, scenarios, and well-rehearsed scripts, and each with its chorus of critics. Contextuality contributes to any proper interpretation of custom and morality, and hence of communication too.

Whatever one tribe regards as outlandish belongs to some other's accepted display. That disapproving word, "outlandish," simply means "foreign," after all!

Yet context implies more than country. A fair working estimate of selves and their appearances, of fleshly endowments, age and gender, words and deeds, demands a sense of human geography. Display takes place in no void but a locus with content and structure. Every action observed has a backdrop, every instant a place. Spatial association and connection qualify everything. Chapter 8 will return to this matter. Now let us look at some other sources of Geltung.

The commercial economies now embracing most of the world use money to mediate among working time, land and resources, productive equipment, and goods and services destined for consumption (and display) and thereby interpose an additional and very momentous step between the human habitat and wild nature. A monetary standard enormously simplifies accumulation, vastly beyond what physical storage of even the least perishable goods would permit. Unfortunately, though, neither money nor goods will ever exist in unlimited quantities. The more one person can grab, the less remains for everyone else.

At what point does the economic inequality this permits become downright inhumanity? Do we have to resign to the sentence pronounced by Saint Matthew, "For ye have the poor always with you"? Does the unevenness of wealth reflect some universal "law of nature," as some writers have argued? Answers to such questions lead into matters of values, but science offers no firm guide.

Concentration of wealth implies someone's deprivation, both of actual means of subsistence and, invidiously, also of Geltung enough to do better. Those devoid of it, it marginalizes economically, socially, and spatially. That inequality has been the bane of all societies, including the systems that arose in history explicitly committed to finding its remedy.

Possession consists entirely of a social attribution of prerogatives to hold or use or dispose of something. Its validity and practical effectiveness have their only basis in a given culture, under its functioning institutions, and specifically in the relevant displays enacted under them. Not entirely fictional, however, such substantive utterance enforces the reality of property, and people hence argue their claims with great determination. Not surprisingly the law, at least in Western lands, speaks mainly the language of money. Why else should we have so many prosperous lawyers?

Some significant part of the blame for great disparities of wealth can be laid to advantages granted to favored positions within the total spatial matrix of societies. As will be explained more at length in Chapter 10, admission to the guarded precincts where the higher echelons of hierarchy conduct their transactions, and whence they issue their commands, seldom fails to coincide with opportunities of gain. Any privileged entry to places where power concentrates in fact can facilitate accumulation. Control of initiative conferred by preferential access to communication networks brings similar benefits. Insiders profit, outsiders go begging.

Even more important, control of the means of production (of information, even more than of objects, as a preceding chapter has pointed out) enables an individual or class to dictate the terms of their use and thereby to siphon off a share of the proceeds from labor. That is the keystone of Marx's whole argument.

Surely accumulation may also express itself, in an altogether tangible fashion, as the conspicuous concentration of valued possessions at residential, recreational, or business sites. The association of power with wealth that this often betokens comes through in the way that people refer to the ornate dwellings of the very rich as "palaces." When people allude to "the empires of commerce," they also tinge them with power.

The opulence decorating certain landscapes proclaims that they belong to the favored, exclusive universe of circulation of an elevated social level, reserved not alone to the wealthy but likewise to the powerful and certain other prominent celebrities. The displays of the rich need proper appreciation and invite their own envious and fawning admirers, not hard to come by. Luxury as much as misery loves company.

Wealth can be only debatably taken for merit. But whenever perceived as a key to and motor of enterprise as well as frivolous ostentation, it enables its holders to bring about change in the physical world of production. This circumstance sometimes signifies all too much for the human custody and conservation of the earth as a livable home. It counts as one of the major problems this book is designed to address (see Chapter 13).

Under appropriate social conditions, the mobilization and direction of human energies toward new technological goals earn credit equivalent to that redounding to the social prominence achieved with the aid of mere idle show. Ever loftier office towers and constantly more sprawling crop fields and factories can vie as personal testimonials with any memorial that people have ever created. At times, moreover, sterile and wasteful monuments to vanity command more Geltung than socially fruitful ones. Egotistic display is the bane of development.

But suitable social conditions are vital for any substantial enterprise, and these are spatial conditions as well, traced out and sustained by communication. Communicative circumstances always contribute their part to any human undertaking. The milieu makes action appear as legitimate.

Indispensable sensitivity to individual display and its Geltung subsumes an acute awareness of features inserted by human work into landscape. Any such element whatsoever may be invoked to count as display. It communicates something when heeded, if only the possible identity of whoever put it in place. It is hard to resist wondering who laid out the mysterious designs on the arid surface of the desert in Peru. More generally, though, any and all anthropogenic contributions to the local landscape scene tend to say more. They declare the pretensions and prerogatives of those who created them. The fragrant old-fashioned *Misthaufen*, or manure pile, in a German farmyard proclaimed a certain degree of prosperity and did not go unremarked. It downright reeked of comparative wealth.

Furthermore, all the walls of the world are political. Awareness of certain facilities in landscape can even exercise power of a sort by restricting initiative and thus reserving it for their builders. Like that of the ostentatious heap of dung in a *Bauernhof*, or farmyard, to which a fastidious passerby will give wide berth, the potency of artificial landscape features serving for political display exceeds by far their latent influence on traffic. This book appraises as essentially political whatever utterance, that is, display, can exert an influence on the behavior of those who perceive it and heed it. Along with gestures and words, the very environment can speak the language of authority. Landscape too is provocative.

And landscapes as well as all sorts of objects themselves come to carry their Geltung. Through their observable association with power and wealth, and perhaps also esthetic appeal, they all can serve as displays, always ready for invocation in dialog, and therefore impressive to those comprehending them. Challenging eloquence belongs as incontrovertibly to autos, houses, and high-rise office buildings as to speech—not to mention woven penis sheaths in New Guinea and clay-clotted coiffures in Zambia. In particular, the lavishness with which a people embellish their temples and shrines, or adorn their sacred sites or cities with graven images and other memorials, betrays almost a compulsion to proclaim the community's values and allegiances by means of constructed displays.

The Geltung Hypothesis can provide a reasonable explanation for the foregoing influential uses of display in landscape. In accord with its premises, the creation of landscapes through alteration of, and addition to, physical features deserves recognition as an art form in its own right. Indeed, the emergence of a distinct profession of landscape design (or landscape architecture) bears witness to this fact. Moreover, any individual who manipulates materials creatively in order to contrive an expressive exhibit works as an artist of sorts. The regular rhythmic pattern of the giant leaves that clothe a Pygmy lean-to bespeaks a more than accidental attention to gratifying, provocative form. Similarly, simply the wealth of cultivated flowering plants so striking in impoverished Third World villages attests to a certain artistry, for many of the species concerned lack practical uses. In fact perhaps art underlies all human display.

It is not the landscape designer or architect alone, then, who makes of a landscape a unique cohesive statement; both whole communities and ordinary individuals, within the modest compass of their powers, do so too. Like any other human undertaking, such elaboration of displays is costly as expenditure of energy and substance, affordable only if efficacious in promoting the welfare of the individual or group. From the ecological standpoint, efforts invested in landscape display figure as installment payments on survival. Let them not be misspent! If such adornments of the local scene do not enhance the prospects of their makers by prompting propitious responses, they simply cost too much—in monetary terms or any other. As any gardener or decorator knows, those displays themselves do always exact some sort of sacrifice. And sacrifice itself is a telling form of display.

The sometimes fearsome festivals mentioned earlier, in Chapter 3, all share a number of features. They center on great convocations and highly formalized activities. They closely conform to and exemplify the crowning themes of the culture concerned, mythical, moral, and material. They flourish on solemn sacrifice.

Each solemnity constitutes a major rite of passage, commonly one centering upon the chief officiant or performer, and each contributes to that person's status, and sometimes to that of dependents. In every case the setting, the venue, proclaims the importance of the event and its actors. They become part of a history told and repeated. And glory resounds far and wide.

Tame testimonial dinners, fund-raising bashes, political rallies, and innumerable other ceremonies regularly observed in North America continue the tradition of potlatch in some degree. They exalt the Gel-

tung of an individual or sometimes a group through a bit of formal behavior combined with festivity observing its own particular etiquette,
and they often call for some token sacrifice, such as donations or presents. Furthermore they tend almost to distil and decant the very essence
of the prevailing general culture.

Modern societies also on occasion practice monster solemn, sacrificial public ceremonials connected with Geltung that greatly exceed in
ferocity and sanguinariness the most unappetizing of the Mayan or
Maori rituals. Boastful pronouncements attend them, great hosts of
people assemble for them, conspicuous waste prevails, and spectacular
violence constitutes their theme. I am speaking of wars. The ominous
problem they pose for humanity also has roots deep in Geltung display.
That fact urgently deserves consideration in the search for a cure to this
deadly human proclivity.

People perhaps do not like to admit that a war is a high ceremonial.
Yet just consider the way it proceeds. Two adversary nations or alliances
muster their armies into a discipline unfamiliar in civilian life, establishing a comprehensive, compulsory hierarchical order expressed and enforced through the clearly ritual behavior exacted by so-called military
courtesy. Spaces undergo a thoroughgoing hierarchial apportionment
among the component, graded authority systems. Everyone puts on a
uniform to signify standing. The armies accumulate their lethal para-
phernalia, which will make up the furnishings for venues of the performance and become its instruments.

As with the potlatch, getting ready for war takes a lot of planning,
preparation, and protocol. Not merely must the authorities accomplish
all the tasks set forth in the previous paragraph, however. Partners have
to be selected and invitations issued and accepted—remember the all
too whimsical question, "What if they gave a war and nobody came?"
And then the big event commences. In an odd illocutionary fashion,
one side begins shooting; the other responds to the provocation, almost
as if to a question. Thereupon everyone shoots and bombs and blows
things up, and people get killed and cities obliterated. The murderous
dialog makes a truly dramatic display, indeed—the biggest show we ever
put on.

O glorious war! The Geltung flows faster and thicker than blood.
Reputations are staked, reputations are made. Sacrifice beckons to everyone. An ideal of heroism prevails, such that people gratefully receive
the grand opportunity to suffer and die as stoically as Mayan kings or
Muslim martyrs, and to hurt as pitilessly as torturers. Each cultural system involved attempts to validate its own virtues while vilifying those of

opponents. The nations engaged can wallow in myopic, unreflective, self-indulgent pride, regardless of battlefield outcomes; by their own received definitions of sacrifice and heroism, even the defeated army and nation almost always find something to boast about. People fight wars not only to win; they fight to be glorious, too.

All this competitive display requires an enormous amount of skilled cooperation among belligerents on both sides, vastly more than a potlatch or any comparable ceremony conceivably could call for. A war's preliminaries put great stress on finesse. Accordingly, starting a war may require almost as much so-called diplomacy as preventing or stopping one does.

The combatants thereupon must follow explicit "rules of the game" in order to carry out their respective programs of death and destruction, lest the enemy fail to appreciate the correctness and legitimacy of the display, God forbid. The courtliness that characterized the wars of the French with the English centuries ago has diminished, but niceties continue de rigueur, at least at the upper levels of command. I recall that the American general in Germany whose unit captured Hermann Goering next day invited him to lunch.

War is all spatially structured, shot through with display, deeply political, ceremonial, social and collaborative, as well as centered on Geltung private and public. Information flies around wildly, in the forms either of commands and reports, or propaganda, or extravagant rumors or simply of bullets and missiles and bombs that say plenty. War has all the earmarks of standard human communication, out of scale and out of normal rational control. Enough has been said by now here about that nightmare habit of the human species to have made the point. Let us quickly turn to more peaceable themes.

A general triumphant in war acquires a good name and to the bane of political prudence becomes almost automatically eligible to stand for high office. Harry Truman wrote that generals make the worst presidents; he had been only a captain. But certain presidents, and prime ministers too, have appeared to use wars to favor their own reelection.

Not every improbable good name derives from such costly expedients, however. An individual's name can allude indirectly also to some of the other attributes mentioned in the course of this essay, and accordingly constitute influential Geltung display. "Names and natures do often agree," goes the proverb. Ominously, though, as other ones warn, "He that hath an ill name is half-hanged," and declare, "Take away my good name and take away my life."

People cultivate face, or impressions, and equally names, or reputations. In the one case direct, in the other far diffused, both portray a personal character. Face is something possessed but not owned. It cannot be litigated or negotiated. Any attempt to expostulate about one's blunders and poor appearances invites ridicule. Excuses and, especially, angry retort only further deepen the shame. A face in disgrace can only be salvaged by later redeeming displays.

In contrast, a name even legally constitutes property. People can sue over defamation, libel, or slander. They can claim damages for unauthorized use of their names. And throughout history, in many cultures, bloody deeds have avenged a slur on a name.

Names also can warp people's images. I do not refer to the mishap of having a hated baptismal name, or even to that of carrying an unpronounceable or comical family name. People also can inflict atrocious ones on themselves by choice, as official changes of name in the newspapers show. In particular, I wish to cite a most curious practice I have discovered through assiduous scanning of 182 North American telephone books (Wagner, 1992). Call it the "Z-phenomenon." As of the year 1990, the final residential listings showed a total of 108 purported family names that began with more than one "Z," distributed over forty-one cities and towns. Sometimes they sported weird initial-Z given names that matched. The number of uninterrupted Z's beginning the last names extended from two to ten. A couple of factors appeared influential: size of the city and Sunbelt location. Los Angeles, of course, could boast the only name that started with ten Z's.

Serious questions arise about these seemingly trivial or frivolous displays. Did each case indicate an independent invention, or had diffusion played a hand? And are the names real? Do their perpetrators and possessors actually write them on their income tax returns? How do they sign their checks? What real Geltung might such names be able to collect?

I continue to wonder what Z-names say about the cultures of North America. Do they ever occur anywhere else? What do they intimate about the tension between the impulse to conform and the tendency to advertise oneself? between the ostensible and intimate selves? between caprice and calculation?

It comes as somewhat startling to encounter systematic aberrations such as these among the customs of familiar places. Minor eccentricities do not astound us, but repeated so consistently and widely, they pose puzzles. Always ready to exculpate aliens for their ridiculous displays, we show less charity toward noncomformists here at home. Surely other peoples similarly judge their own more harshly than they do the stranger.

Culture, though, does not go far enough toward explanation of the individual's activities and shows. Behavior stems from deeper roots. Ever-secret inner impulse rises in expression. Display does not explain itself. We must read its texts without footnotes.

The ways in which people can score against the scales embodied in Geltung consist of tiny inventions, modest innovations in their behavior, that bid for attention. Any extreme in display tends to arouse some notice, but the response will certainly not be positive in every case. Some behavior alarms us, some of it distresses us, and some is downright repugnant. Conversely, other shows interest us, charm us, or entice us to emulate. A "zero" response, total indifference, is the one thing that display abhors. An experienced politician once allegedly advised a neophyte contender that "it doesn't matter at all what people say about you, just get them to talk a lot about you." High fashion designers and their more daring clients likewise subscribe to this maxim.

Things can go too far, however, or not far enough. The maximum Geltung doesn't reward the maximum display. Conversely, too little liveliness, too little novelty, also impair the effect. It takes sensitivity to gauge just the right amount of originality and vividness to suit the particular audience. The tailor must tailor the suit to others besides the wearer.

People's reactions to the Geltung of any kind of display, whether positive or negative, remain always relative, all a matter of degree. We can seldom acknowledge either perfection or absolute worthlessness, although we take note of plenty of mediocrity and insignificance, and everything in between the far extremes. Every individual acts to register as high as possible on the scale of esteem and respect, or at least to securely pass muster. People tend to try to "give it all that they've got" in display in appropriate venues, for the purpose of maximizing standing and prerogatives within the society.

Is Geltung a matter of unbridled, strictly personal competition? Not quite. Although it clearly rests on comparison among displays, despite its relevance to social rank Geltung accrues to the displays as such, not to persons expressly. An unknown cut-up in the crowd needs no name to become objectionable. The displays must be highly selective, not only presented when and where they do the most good, but also, in order to sustain a reputation, constantly either repeated or varied in order to maintain an advantageous impression. That is why we all have our secrets and shield ourselves from unflattering exposure. We resist full disclosure: outbursts of resentment and revenge come down on the heads of the peeper or tattler. A cat can look at a king well enough and notice no clothes, but woe betide whoever else has so much temerity as to notice royal nakedness. Off with their heads!

In fact, all we cats ought to look well at our kings. "Curiosity killed a cat," they say, but lack of curiosity must have killed vastly more.

Persistent and shrewd attention to impressions created—that is, an eye for the audience—can obviously profit a person. A good reputation counts as a precious possession, and people will cherish and defend it as doggedly as anything owned. Demeanor and dress in themselves do not simply profess a certain claim to deference and respect; in addition they may do so as tokens of established reputation. People harvest and hoard and exhibit material marks of distinction—as Pierre Bourdieu (1979) describes it—that derives not so much from the novelty of their display per se as from its association with prestigious institutions and social groups. The uniform insignia marks apart the officer and gentleman/gentlema'am. Clothing vests wearers with reputations.

Sartorial evidence of claims to a good reputation also includes the fabric quality and the cut of the raiment. Three-piece suits make business people convincing, while sneakers, jeans, and T-shirts spell "out of place in the office" except when computer wizards are wearing them.

Reputation, fashion, fame, and even wealth and power and love, are at base no more than terms for particular tones of responding display, and the inner states we can only infer from the latter. All of them manifest themselves solely as interpreted through reactions garnered from provocative displays. All of them are relative, too; they depend upon systems in space and in time.

Reputations may circulate as far as given information fields extend, although often the cultural differentiation of the respective receivers modifies their evaluation from place to place. A successful headhunter, much admired in the tribe, may not go over so well in New York (but then these days, who knows?). Restriction of the circulation of a reputation to particular institutional networks also limits the rewards it can earn. A prelate revered by some arcane sect may have to wait at the back of the grocery line and suffer the taunts of the kids on the block.

And the estimate that circulates about a person has likewise a definite political aspect. Besmirch an aspirant's reputation and you wipe out a candidacy; impugn a suitor's sincerity and parents and friends will (probably fruitlessly) caution the deceived beloved. The notoriously political effects of diffused reactions to a person enter strongly into deals of all sorts, too. The "heavyweights" can get things done and get things they want. A famous entertainer, a financial mogul, or a top nuclear scientist will enjoy preferential access to the halls of the mighty. Similar privilege on occasion even gives entry to the bedrooms of the beautiful. "Power is a great aphrodisiac," as Henry Kissinger supposedly said.

The question for the next chapter then must be, How do people face up to multiple Geltung criteria?

SEVEN

• Selective Impressions

People sometimes may ask you, searchingly, what you see in some person, what you have heard about them, what they have to show for the chances they've had. As the German phrase puts it, what do you "hold of them"?

Outside the charmed circles of friendship and love, attention, acceptance, and manifest approval or admiration have to be earned the hard way. Many varied sorts of display—of the body, property, deportment, or location—may yield their degrees of positive Geltung. Conversely, the same dimensional scale permits of contrary judgments. Aware of it or not, everyone walks in a limelight all the time, however dim its illumination. Attentive eyes and ears scan for the provocations any person constantly displays, and tongues are ever ready to wag, fingers to point, and arms to embrace or to thrust away.

The multiplicity of possible witnesses renders any actual display in effect ambivalent and even a little risky, for what goes over with one interlocutor need not sit well with the next. Venue has to validate performance; culture and individual standpoint furnish the standards of judgment. In such an awkward situation, people have to take their chances with their presentations. "The drama's laws the drama's patrons give," intoned Samuel Johnson, "for we that live to please must please to live."

But whatever the hazards, people have to interact with and display to others. When "it's all in the family" or "just among friends," a presentation is easiest. But at large in the world, the rule is to "put your best foot forward." How does an individual learn which foot to start dancing with, and with which to start marching? By imitation, surely, and with coaching, as always.

Vocabularies of display, as of speech itself, grow in that manner, tested and refined and personalized with time. Embroidered with attention-getting, gratifying variations, each incident of display incurs the notice or neglect, approval or reprobation of its witnesses, and their reactions to it will militate strongly for or against its repetition. Three cheers for a lucky first shot, but also thank God for mistakes! How else would any-one ever learn very much?

To put it another way, communicative acts fall subject to a kind of "natural" selection just as rigorous, perhaps, as the pressure that ruth-lessly sorts out genetic mutations. Seldom does it kill, but it frequently wounds, and teaches thereby. The net effect of selection of dialog dis-plays, over a generous span of time, inculcates deportment adapted to the milieu. Or else it so severely deprives and impairs the individual that it can often induce eventual perceptual distortions and bizarre behav-ioral symptoms. A subsequent section discusses such communicative ab-errations that register negative social selection. But what does that kind of selection have to do with sheer survival, with natural selection in the strict sense?

If nature does impose on humanity an "ecological imperative," de-manding suspension of territoriality in favor of sociality, plus imitative learning and liberated circulation; and if, as a feature of the human na-ture ordained by this, enhanced communicative vigor and versatility have to furnish the means of overcoming spatial tensions, greatly foster-ing lifelong imitative learning and empowering human beings to col-laborate constantly; and furthermore, if enhanced communication must in turn depend upon personal Geltung: if all these premises be just, then the pressures of nature itself would surely select without mercy against an individual bereft of all Geltung—denied participation in society, de-prived of a human education, lacking communicative competence, and unsuited hence for collaborative action.

It might be supposed that few if any human beings normally corre-spond to such a dire specification. How can anyone talk of a natural selection working on people here in our world and our time? Common humanity, we tell ourselves, promises some portion of mercy and con-cern for almost anyone. Yet the present (1995) plight of the Bosnians, Somalis, Afghans, Ruandans, and Haitians shows that compassion and charity also fall short. Peoples remote and unfamiliar fail to stir fellow feeling strongly enough; even the Geltung of societies can be decisive. And so a cruel selection takes place, primarily preying on those possessing minimal Geltung in their own communities: women and children, the aged, the humble—the passive, unarmed, or powerless ones. At best, they have to live in want and obscurity; at worst, they may perish from starvation, exposure, or violence in payment for their guiltless insignificance.

An infinitely less drastic but still relentless selection occurs in everyone's everyday life. People may chalk their defeats and disappointments up to luck, or blame other people for their woes, but more often the fault lies with themselves, or rather with the way they manifest themselves to others. However, such a fault consists merely of some infelicitous communicative performance in its cultural context, and not of either a moral shortcoming or a natural, innate defect. Yet, although the world's professed standards still do appear to discriminate unreasonably and unjustly, a person in a less-wracked land can hope at least to survive if adept at appropriate display.

Some suitable manner of display almost always exists for cheating too severe a selection. The jester in the court could tell the king a thing or two; Scheherazade foiled her captor by telling clever tales. Pious individuals set forth as pilgrims to holy sites to atone very visibly for their sins. Likewise conspicuous courage has sometimes gained a chivalrous reprieve for defeated commanders. Wit and charm, grace and gallantry, wisdom or notable skills can often compensate in part for poverty and powerlessness. Conversely, wealth and political influence do very nicely as substitute trumps when absolutely all the saving attributes mentioned are glaringly absent in their lucky possessors. An alert and prudent individual therefore watches for ways of mustering Geltung and constantly tests their effectiveness.

Display, according to the Geltung Hypothesis, solicits response of a kind that promotes the social and hence the ecological survival of the individual. It both fuels and lubricates the mechanisms of dialog. Admittance to places and conversations, demonstrated influence within them, and resounding echoes thereof in reputational diffusion, meter its effectiveness. Those external signs and sanctions serve to shape the public behavior of individuals sagacious enough to attend to them.

Selection for successful patterns of utterance, involving elimination of the inefficacious ones, however, does not operate automatically, according simply to the responses forthcoming. The outward outcomes of encounters register inwardly again, and covert processes of mind evalu-

ate that evidence and formulate adjustment to it. Whatever the modifications ensuing, reactions in dialog still continue their pressure. Thus a
person's unsparingly realistic appraisal of results can help to ensure fe-
licitous communication. But the tenderness of ego most often denies
what the eyes can plainly see. Being totally honest with oneself is the
hardest honesty of all.

Impatient ambition at once both feeds anxiety and nourishes treacherous equanimity in facing the reception of one's own behavior. Thus
self-delusion and insensibility tend to enter into habitual choices, and
people find themselves fixed into routines not fully propitious for Geltung. Presumably, social selection would most favor those individuals
able to maximize the positive reactions to their net displays, or to optimize their consequences for pursuit of particular purposes. But a part of
the gratification gained from responses consists of emotional payoffs that
may or may not reflect the external situation faithfully. Fools find a para-
dise easily.

Nevertheless, no matter how blindly and awkwardly, people seem
programmed innately to try as best they can to optimize or maximize
their social viability. Deep internal promptings tell them how, whether
or not they faithfully follow them. Ambition recoils from affronts and
anxiety answers them. Shame, often betrayed in demeanor, follows transgressions and derelictions detectable by others. The face of guilt gives
secret misgivings away. Alone inside, the monitor tirelessly watches and
warns.

Psychologists posit a private self-image informing behavior, but know-
able to others, of course, only through highly fallible conjectures based
on manifest display. The public feedback and communicated reputation
that constantly assess everyone's actions exert great selective long-term
effects, but so do inward emotions and excitations responding to them.
People strive not to "forget themselves," that is, their public selves or
personas, in the presence of others. Evidently, individuals do maintain
an image of self of some kind, for they seem to be forever tinkering and
toying with it and testing it out in the world.

Routinized and relatively inconsequential acts of display make up the
overwhelming majority. Those regular, unspectacular expressions, however, ordinarily much exceed in number and intensity the minimal
quantity and quality required for sustaining a social identity and involvement in shared activities. People interact for interaction's sake and express themselves just in order to express themselves. However, such
activities, despite their apparent superfluity, in fact do serve an indis-

pensable function. Nothing less than inveterate testing can feed enough information back to the individual's monitor faculty in order to organize behavior well according to ever-changing contexts and conditions. Expression is a window into other lives, a mirror in front of our own.

The self as sole agent of the maximization of its own advantage has to make the most of advance and adaptive information in order to steer behavior toward success. That requires a guidance beyond spontaneous, unconfirmed impulse. In order to gather reliable information on possible reactions of other people, individuals must venture somewhat bold displays. Always taking a chance, they probe for acceptable and efficacious novelty. Else the information content remains only slight.

Try what you can and see how it works: that is the rule of contingency imposed on all behavior. But trying and testing in security, before necessity bears down, reduce the ultimate risks. Playing teaches. A large part of life is rehearsal for actual living.

Play is the pleasantest school. Ego is always star pupil, and every companion a teacher. The lessons teach about self, the powers and joys of the body, as well as of things in the world and their uses. Yet if simply playing alone, children or anyone else will learn but a small part of living, for only company puts them in touch with the social side of themselves. Only together can people develop the skills of cultivating appearances in order to cultivate people.

However, a child requires just a little coaching before catching on. Every infant begins its induction into communicative society within the family, exerting with its first hiccups and cooing and crying an imperious sway over caregivers. Mothers, gifted with an acute sensitivity to any signal from the infant slung on their backs or laid in the crib, attend with alacrity to their offspring's demands. The infant acquires a good taste of Geltung right then!

As they grow, those obligate addicts of Geltung, exuberant children at play cry out, in the literal sense, for attention. They scream, "Hey, watch me!" as they clamber and tumble and shamelessly pose. How could a kid learn riding a bike without saying, "Look, Dad! No hands!" and taking a spill? Play craves dialog.

Children moreover, ad hoc, improvise miniscule societies and cultures. The light-hearted yet earnest business of children, highly vocal and gestural, resounds with negotiations of status and with rules and constant debate over rules. Even play can be highly political.

Much has been written of play in regard to its role in developing skills and nurturing talents in children. Play among the "higher" animals, too, has been recognized as instrumental and vital in their learning to survive. Some writers have even gone so far as to say that "life is a game," and to mean it. But that goes too far. Play is protected and tentative, free in the main of the penalties real life imposes. Play, only training, forgives.

Who else but a child—or a billionaire or a vicious tyrant—would ever get away with the greedy possessiveness children are wont to reveal? Who else except an idiot could speak with such crushing candor? What other sort of person save a warped torturer would delight in inflicting such pain as a child unconcernedly may on animals, comrades, and oftentimes parents? Nonage alone permits such improprieties to go (sometimes) unpunished, all on behalf of the learning involved.

In most instances, sooner or later, painful experience instills inhibitions on infantile beastliness, after all. Imitative learning and its costlier counterpart, selective inhibitive learning on a trial-and-error basis, shape activity into behavior acceptable socially. The offences just cited are social, and learning through either experiment with or example from peers efficiently programs a child for more-harmonious adult behavior. Necessarily—and fortunately—play produces mostly conformists, although it cannot abolish the underlying evil potentialities that lurk within every human individual and sometimes burst forth when social pressures relent.

Adults also play in their fashion, although far less wildly and joyously than their offspring. In the exquisitely subtle give and take among players, they often form and improve their estimates of their companions. The lesson they learn most eagerly of all, but not always rightly, is that of how others regard them (or, God forbid, disregard them). If blessed with realistic, tough humility, they also can learn a lot about themselves. At any stage of life, play tests Geltung under a truce. Infractions of order and poor performances generally, although subject to monitory comment, get off lightly. Only when physical or monetary pain is inflicted may matters become uncomfortable. In fact a prudent person will welcome the opportunity to play, and hardly just for idle distraction.

When human beings play, then, they indulge themselves in every level of learning. As much as any other activity of living creatures, human play is also a compulsive quest for information. It teaches about the physical world, its astonishing contents and their geographies; it teaches much about people—to themselves and to others; and likewise it teaches how to operate more and more effectively within that physical context and human society. Not the least of its lessons, by any means, instructs in propitious communication through display as fortified by personal Geltung.

All very well: people test. Try before you buy. But like rumpled, ill-fitted folk who never seem to comprehend clothes, some people appear unable to learn from a test. Obsessed with some unique pathway toward Geltung, they never abate in their singular blind pursuit. Oblivious of circumstances, such people translate whatever situation they encounter into terms of their own. Rebuffs do not phase them and rewards fail to satiate them.

Look for example at people impatient always to be first with whatever is latest, incapable of resting easy with any but the very newest fashion or fad in food or finery, in home decorations or vacation spots. They hasten to discard whatever has served to grab a moment of attention and rush to grasp for the next novel lure. Such people trade their serenity for shows of whatever is most strikingly recent.

Evidently, trendy people do not really need the novelties they sport; the pedant seeks for impressions, not enlightenment; great seducers quest merely for endless conquests, not love or even frank physical rapture. But two particular obsessive types occasion far more pain and harm than any other annoying but trivial sort. People who have sipped the intoxicant of great personal influence and gotten drunk on the taste cannot often refrain from draining it down to the dregs. What they pursue without pause or moderation matters because it involves everyone. History and literature show the way such vanity leads often toward madness. And all the world, always and everywhere, is full of wasted sacrifices to its idols. Power-crazed people will wither our world for their vanities, and are doing so now.

The craving for either great influence or simply wealth can seize individuals obsessively and enormously exceed a reasonable care for comfort and security. It makes tyrants or misers of some, recluses of many, and all it imprisons in fear and mistrust. The work and worry of the mighty and rich never cease, however much envy surrounds them. And still, both influentiality and riches exhilarate and embolden, adding an unwholesome zest to the struggle to accumulate yet more and blotting out consciousness of the consequences.

Wealthy and powerful individuals are able to indulge subsidiary ambitions. Seldom, for one thing, are people with power reluctant to take advantage of their positions to enrich themselves, and the wealthy willingly employ their resources to intervene in politics and public affairs. Through both acquisitions and benefactions, they intrude their influence so far as into the arts. Even mere stars of entertainment and sport are not at all averse to pursuing great wealth, and sometimes power as well. Perhaps the saddest symptom of the discontent and failure truly to fulfill themselves afflicting prominent people declares itself in desperate search for genuine love and trustworthy friendship. Hard always to come by, those prizes too easily elude the people who themselves are tantalizing prizes for predatory schemers.

All the burdensome obsessions mentioned are outgrowths of longing for Geltung. All of them fester in cultural context, and all the celebrity they pursue, all the advantages they can secure, consist of nothing more than the fruits of communication. And the very positions they crave are objective locations somewhere on earth (never in Heaven!) and depend as much on the Geltung attributed to those places as on anything more tangible.

So the very foundations of humanity's peculiar adaptation, employing intensive and versatile communication driven by cravings for Geltung, are also the sources of obsession and vanity. Moreover, the degree of the spatial connection, control, and privilege that particular individuals acquire through this normal behavior of the species gives them vast scope for affecting the world around them. Vain and obsessive behavior, if they occur, then become dangerous. My argument, once fully spelled out in the ensuing chapters, will maintain that the inordinate powers thus mustered and easily misapplied largely account for humanity's gravest dilemmas and dangers, fully as much as for its remarkable successes.

The distorting and disruptive effects of an immoderate urge for Geltung and the longing for spatial autonomy reach even into individual lives and family circles. Despite their indispensable contribution to human ecological success, the two presumably innate tendencies go far toward explaining the personal misadventures and maladaptations that burden a great many human beings.

A mere obsession with fame, wealth, power, or fashion can count as comparatively bearable, if not socially beneficial, no matter how vain. However, when personal Geltung sinks so low that all society seems to reject or ignore an individual persistently, a crisis is likely to ensue. Ambition and anxiety gnaw at self-confidence. Normal intercourse with people becomes burdensome. Faith falters. Dysfunctional compensatory behavior often develops in the individual. Social bonds become strained beyond tolerance.

The scope of this book clearly does not extend to social pathology or psychiatric afflictions. However, the bare realities of obvious distress and compensations for it frequently seem to correlate well with personal Geltung deficiencies. This warrants a short and necessarily fairly inexpert consideration here of some of them.

The communicative matrices in which an individual is most involved—"primary reference groups," in the sociologist's terms—can prove extremely uncongenial and persistently detract from performance displayed. Trouble in school and educational failure may for this reason indicate dissociation from the networks and milieus, and therefore the standards and practices, that prevail within the official system. Opposing or peripheral associations may accord greater positive Geltung in return for less effort and embarrassment than the classroom does. Express rejection of the latter's values may earn Geltung in the dissident circle, whose own alternative activities become the arenas of achievement and advancement. The truants dominate spaces and connections inaccessible to others, and their territoriality confirms a unique identity that pupils herded into classes cannot hope for. The excitement and glamor of delinquent life make more than a match for dull schooling.

Dropouts, delinquents, and downright criminals reject the regular standards of institutional systems in favor of rules accepted by their own spontaneous institutions. As groups, they create their own autonomous networks of communication and command, with corresponding audience constellations. They develop distinctive political realms and hierarchies analogous to those of other social elements.

Yet by no means does their secession from conventional society grant them license to act in any way that they please; the codes they have to obey are if anything tighter and less gentle. In compensation, perhaps, the adversarial relationship with police and other official agencies lends zest and adventure to their lives, bringing ample opportunity for daring and prowess earning Geltung. Territorial rivalries among the various organized groups make life all the more precarious and promise proportionate rewards. Both serious criminal activity and dropout delinquency share such common features.

Chicago's fabled gangster wars of the 1930s find echoes in the current skirmishes of deprived urban youth. No city anywhere lacks parasitic, predatory bands, whereas rural areas may harbor bandits, and pirates infest the tropical seas. The juvenile and young adult gangs of big cities in America respond to compelling attractions inherent in all such situations. The traffic in drugs or arms or stolen goods they often conduct brings plenty of easy money. They exalt combat virtues and talents that take a high toll in young lives. But they also provide solidarity and trust that may be lacking in the actual families that often continue to feed their members, at least in more prosperous countries.

Such disaffected outsider groups revert, in a sense, to more primitive levels of conduct, emphasizing rigid spatial restrictions and extolling predation and violence. At the cost of renouncing social position and respectability they promise respect to society's rejects.

Comparable symptoms of withdrawal and reorientation go with addictions. Beleaguered, Geltung-starved people may discover a refuge in alcohol, which increases the ostensible spontaneity of action and dampens and distorts the resulting feedback. Confirmed alcoholics tend finally to drift away from family and home and seek the company of kindred spirits along Skid Roads, or sometimes merely in country clubs. Thus, losing their grip on the networks they formerly favored and served, and unwelcome at home, they too often adopt a new spatial context and a new subcultural milieu.

For related reasons, drug addiction shows similar but even more severe features. In its own bizarre fashion, it too dulls and transforms perception, inducing anything from pleasurable passivity to mild euphoria to manic exuberance, all more or less exempt from sensitivity to censure and Geltung deprival. "Spaced out," the drug user enters another reality, which finally tends to resemble a personal prison.

Only a short step separates addiction from chronic mental malfunction. Vulgar usage sometimes accurately describes the victims as "not all there." Both communicative aberrations and spatial abnormalities—disconnection from present surroundings, inveterate wandering, or even total immobility—commonly characterize psychological illnesses. The worlds the patients live in differ from those of the rest of humanity by enough to render them more convincing, at least, than what lies outside, but they need not be pleasant or congenial. Terrifying delusions may haunt their darknesses. In certain cases those subjective worlds may indulge the patients by permitting assumption of fancied identities loaded with spurious positive Geltung, but fear and crushing guilt may just as readily afflict the victims within.

Psychosomatic illnesses might presumably arise for analogous reasons. They afford a selective and opportune rescue from embarrassment and inconvenience by disabling and hence excusing an individual from participating in unpropitious communicative situations and visiting threatening places, and furthermore furnish displays that elicit sympathetic Geltung. Sometimes, as well, their very symptoms intelligibly dramatize the conflicts or inhibitions that bother the victim. Akin to these cases are those where spatial vulnerabilities, such as agoraphobia and acrophobia, markedly restrict mobility and thereby obviate some sort of feared experience. How many additional psychiatric afflictions might focus on Geltung and space?

When entangled in networks that too much restrict their mobility, subject them to controls they resent, or hamper their Geltung or livelihood prospects, people thus either confect a more congenial perceptual setting with which they can deal or attempt in various ways to disengage and reposition themselves, as detailed above. The refractory student drops out of school; the reprobate drunkard leaves home; the resentful employee mired in a tedious job without promise abandons it. People will go to any extremes to find a place for themselves and a promise of Geltung.

Vast numbers of rural folk desert the stagnant, starving countryside in order to take their chances among the barrios and bidonvilles of Third World cities. Immigrants, legal or otherwise, swarm into prosperous countries from war-torn and poor ones. They seek freedom, opportunity, and safety. But security, scope for advancement, and personal liberty are primarily the consequences of enhanced communicative relationships. And whatever constraints and disadvantages impel an individual to move most often involve a correspondingly oppressive and restrictive communicative ambiance. The galling negativity of typical reactions to either impoverished nonentity or flagrant nonconformity ought to suffice to drive away anyone able to flee, quite apart from actual survival considerations. The pressures probably originate as much in an excess of derogatory, domineering communicative responses constantly experienced as in calm calculations of material advantage. People escaping a place also escape from a personal image, from poverty of Geltung.

Predicaments a good deal less demeaning also frequently revolve around communicative issues, particularly prejudicial overloads of negative responses. Nothing, perhaps, can illustrate this better than marital discord. Contrary to the common assumption, an overabundance of communication, rather than too little, might best explain the estrangement and pain that often devastate families. A constant display of nagging and negative comments, or simply of flagrant disregard, manifests lack of respect and support and undermines concord and confidence. The Geltung granted so lavishly at first by love evaporates in heated contention. The all too expressive partners only then may retreat into sullen silence or defect entirely. Holy acrimony!

The symptomatology of Geltung deprivation and spatial disadvantage could readily extend to many more kinds of cases from everyday life. Nevertheless, the overwhelmingly positive functions of Geltung in releasing the individual and whole social group from spatial restrictions and thus permitting improvement of ecological adaptation deserve the primary emphasis. Humanity's rise to primacy, its worldwide expansion, its persistent genetic unity, its cultural growth through diffusion, its capacity even to cope with natural crises and the threats that it causes itself, all have had to presuppose this singular device. Geltung makes selves. Geltung makes possible human uniqueness. Geltung remakes the world.

Problems of the varied kinds enumerated in this chapter, ranging from despoliation of the habitat to institutional conflict and personal pathologies, while arising out of this element of human nature, likewise throw down a challenge to it to take charge and correct for its own deleterious influence. This discussion will lead on to a brief consideration of the possibilities of beneficial change that might be achieved. But before reaching that point it now must attempt to expose the spatial consequences of human communication for cultural growth and social integration, and the contribution to them of personal Geltung.

EIGHT

• Getting Around

The common law has furnished folk wisdom with an eloquent adage: "Every man's home is his castle." It is only fair to amend it, however, in order to acknowledge the indisputably prior and more profound truth that a woman's home is even more hers, though at times more prison than castle.

Then humans are territorial creatures after all, are they not? Indeed, apparently universally, they delineate and defend their private sectors of space, their home places, in much the same way as do other creatures. Yet if the bounds they set to those private places had been fated to remain inviolate, impermeable, the story of humanity would never have been written, for not only the art of writing but also history itself, and culture as well, would never have come about.

At least three different levels or layers of what may be called personal spatial autonomy can exist. The successively closer confines they mark out surround a human being as well as most "higher" animals, and transgression of any such bounds prompts its own defensive or evasive reaction. The body surface proper; an "envelope" of personal space (well described by Robert Sommer, 1969); and a zone of security determined by what animal behavior specialists call "flight distance" all go along with territoriality in the strict sense to comprise a system of perimeter defenses in depth.

Although, among human beings, casual and brief bodily contact caused by circumstantial crowding usually arouses little protest, it can only enjoy its impunity as long as it remains in effect anonymous, for then it does not constitute unauthorized intimacy and thus become a communicative display, a provocation. The wariness with which strangers avoid acknowledging one another in crowded situations, such as buses and elevators, exemplifies this principle. The privilege of touching another person's body freely and directly otherwise belongs only to a few categories of individuals—parents (up to a certain age of the offspring), lovers, physicians, fellow contestants in sport; else it becomes an impermissible aggression.

Even mere eye contact or close scrutiny of another individual can be taken as a serious offense. In some societies too lingering a gaze invites immediate and violent retaliation. Likewise, eavesdropping on another's private conversation carries risks. But just such sensory address as this, when properly conducted and consented to, is also the indispensable precondition for dialog.

Visual and audial involvements of this kind establish an explicit sensory linkage—switch open a channel—between individuals, something distinct from the intimacy manifested by body contact. It may require some form of highly formalized and constrained physical contact, for example, a handshake or embrace, briefly held, in order to commence proceedings. Such corporal formalities serve a purely communicative function. The interactional relationship so instituted can be equated with the dyad fundamental to communication.

Relatively unrestricted body contact establishes intimacy, surely by definition itself communicative, although hopelessly difficult to describe and analyze in terms applicable to display in general or discursive utterance. It nevertheless must certainly count as a valid and relevant category of influential communicative behavior. In this connection, the not infrequent tendency of marital partners to seek commercial practitioners of sexual practices they would not propose to their mates exposes an important communicative feature. On the other hand, sensory interactions between individuals at some slight distance apart make up the bulk of the exchanges of sequential displays that most concern this discussion. The zones in which they are consummated usually comprise not a mass of tightly squeezed bodies, of course, but rather a matrix of personal spaces, or invisibly delimited personal bodily "envelopes," the specific dimensions of which depend strikingly, as Edward T. Hall (1956, 1966, 1976) has shown, on the given community concerned. Comfortable conversational proximity means different things to different peoples, in the same way that each given folk permits its own kind of "polite" bodily contact. The respective spatial perimeters of intimacy and social interaction have a third counterpart in a personal zone of security.

The first two of the foregoing three types of spatial units have to do primarily with the regulation of encounters between two human beings, whereas the third also concerns confrontations with other species. Approach beyond the limits of the latter sphere precipitates, among many species, either escape or a fight. When a human individual breaks through the outer bounds of the personal space envelope, similar reactions may take place. However, this third sort of defense perimeter probably retains its effectiveness mainly during meetings with threatening members of other species. And something at least resembling it expresses itself in the prudent detours an individual may take in a city, in order to get around ominous strangers and risky districts.

The home place, finally, represents yet another bastion of individual, and likewise familial, exclusivity. That private preserve, like its three concentric counterparts, fulfills a defensive function. But any one of the respective personal perimeters can be peacefully breached, on condition of appropriate appeasement behavior. A greeting often is asking for something—permission for closer approach.

Territorial precincts of the kind just cited patently present themselves as clearly demarcated landscape features almost everywhere in the world. A cartographer could map them as nested compartments. Nevertheless, another map might show something quite different—a space all transected by networking pathways. Whereas it is private places, cozily claiming their spots in the greater mosaic, that shelter and nurture humanity, what in fact makes humanity human are the connection, interaction, and communication permitted by access to public spaces, over those networks that likewise permeate landscapes.

But overlay the two model maps and you observe the potential for tension. Pathways cross boundaries; any traffic will likely transgress some personal spatial domains, and evidently it indeed cannot avoid doing so frequently. Such a principle might frustrate intercourse and interchange altogether had humanity not hit upon an exceedingly practical palliative: ceremonious amends for transgressions of boundaries.

The sharing of space without special friction gives humanity enormous social and ecological advantages. Some other creatures also on occasion share their spaces, such as the leks where prairie fowl congregate to perform their courtship dances, or the feeding sites sporadically enjoyed in common by many other birds. But none, presumably, carves such essentially "public" spaces out of nesting territories. And under ordinary circumstances, animal incursions into conspecifics' breeding refuges that do not elicit threat displays or induce combat are decidedly rare; the young in particular are just too vulnerable. In contrast, human beings tend to welcome outsiders to their private places, if only properly propitiated.

In addition, the proprietary claims of human territoriality, such as it is, always exempt substantial areas, which then can serve the needs of circulation and encounter: the village pathways, wells, and square, for example. A weak and partial exemption from ranking and rivalry obtains within these public domains, as in the case of domestic dogs too, although, like express violations of private place boundaries, certain encounters might entail violence if not defused by ceremoniality, for they may involve infringements of spaces even more sacrosanct than those of home places.

Certain forms of ceremoniality give license to transgress the bounds of either bodily untouchability, permissible proximity, or prudent distance, as well as the privacy of home places. Foreshadowed weakly in routines of appeasement that prevail among members of rank-ordered animal species, the displays that conditionally suspend human spatial exclusivity employ, like the former, tokens of submission, propitiation, or compensation. Frequent, extremely familiar, yet heeded only when missed, a succession of rather perfunctory observances of spatial etiquette accompanies each human being's daily progression through sectors socially construed, which furthermore are often expressly constructed in solid material form. In this manner, ceremoniality pervades our everyday rounds.

We are constantly knocking on doors, making excuses, begging permission, saying goodbyes, or paying for things. In America, a typical domestic day commences with a bid to rejoin society as upon arising the individual wheezes or grunts acknowledgment of a bedmate; then conducts, with suitable knocks and urgent outcry, the siege of the bathroom; then enters the breakfast assembly by saying "good morning" or commenting on the weather or the burnt toast; then packing off the children to school with kisses and a few appropriate injunctions; and thus departing for work with a peck or a hug and light words. It does not end there; similar token politenesses must continue throughout every waking day, as individuals scrupulously negotiate their entries and exits on itineraries through invisibly and visibly configured space.

The space through which this ceremonial march proceeds consists of discrete social situations, or venues, rather than simply of physically delimited sectors themselves, although constructed facilities tend often to render the two synonymous. The performances used in negotiating passage understandably conform not merely to the minor mechanical tasks entailed, but mainly to the established communicative procedures of the people concerned. Like most of what constitutes social behavior, these usages have their origins in routines acquired through imitative learning, repetitively spread by the process of cultural diffusion that a subsequent chapter will describe. The French shake hands when saying, "Bonjour"; the Japanese bow deeply; yet other peoples rub noses or just embrace warmly; some tribesfolk in New Guinea are even said to salute by touching the genitals. But despite diverse particular formulas, the underlying common theme always embodies a plea for permission to enter or leave someone's company.

Under any particular culture, the routines required all somewhat resemble each other but differ in detail according to the given class of spatial transgression. Close, deliberate touching of certain parts of the body demands different preliminaries than does introduction into a conversation in progress, for example. Inadvertent overstepping of bounds that pertain to one spatial category may dictate symbolic retreat to a more remote one. Unwarranted but accidental intimacy or intrusion thus becomes transmuted into amending conversational interaction. As Erving Goffman so well documented for North American society (1959, 1967, 1970, 1971), numerous expiatory formulas may fulfill such a function.

Mostly, you look but don't touch. Since prerogatives of penetration into any defensive zone surrounding an individual reflect the specific social identity of the intruder with respect to the subject, any augmentation or diminution of those prerogatives must hinge on some modification of that identity. Hence the ceremonious behavior that attends all such spatial and social transgression amounts to small transformations of social and thereby, in effect, of spatial identity. People talk about status and space all the time without knowing it.

Evidently even minor changes of identity involve, indeed require, communication. In accordance with the principles discussed in the foregoing section, they also entail realignment of communicative prerogatives. Thus, altered social relationships both result as consequences of communication and institute new conditions for further communication. Less obvious but equally sure is the fact that the particular displays that bring about such changes also possess, at least ideally, an actual spatial component—contact, encounter, approach; or entry and exit—and in turn confer expressly spatial prerogatives as well.

Recall that to be permitted close, free bodily contact, a dyad partner must acquire the status of an intimate; also that one must be accepted as an interlocutor or associate in order to interact socially; and that the stranger who enters a home assumes the guise of a guest—in each case by means of some ceremonious transaction. In this light, the correspondence and reciprocities among identity, status, or social relationship, on the one hand, and on the other, respectively, the forms of ceremoniality and the incident spatial prerogatives, become plain. Think, for example, of the celebrity who tips the maître d'hôtel generously in order to be seated in a choice and prominent spot in the fashionable restaurant: an even more lavish tip would not secure that coveted place for a ragged nonentity; nor would the seat be gladly given to anyone, however well known, who neglected to say the right words and offer a tip.

"Getting ahead in the world" is often a question of actually moving ahead through the carefully measured ritual spaces of venues. Although the universal importance of ritual status change has long been recognized, its inherent spatial character and implications have not, nor has its communicative basis.

Almost a century ago, Arnold van Gennep (1909) called attention to the worldwide occurrence of solemn ceremoniality attending and confirming passage from each of the successive stages of a human life, as a given people conceives them, into the next. The momentous transitions with which these "rites of passage" are concerned include such as coming into the world at birth; the complementary attainment of motherhood by the woman; enrollment of the infant into the societal universe (e.g., through baptism); initiation rites, to which Christian confirmation and Jewish bar mitzvah correspond; sometimes, betrothal; marriage; induction into the priesthood or military; academic or professional promotion; coronation and ennoblement; and of course death and funerals. Many such occasions are celebrated in parallel fashion in most or all human communities, although some kinds may be confined to a few scattered peoples.

But occasions for rites of passage, in view of the arguments advanced above, can only be infinite. I shall propose that they arise each time an individual anywhere attempts to negotiate a passage across a socially manifested boundary. Van Gennep simply fixed his emphasis on the most spectacular and consequential instances of rites of passage, but his investigation left implications as well for all the more modest ones. Whoever "gets out of line" must be transgressing prohibited boundaries, actual or figurative, without the right ritual leave.

Van Gennep's enlightening study neglected, however, to illuminate the inherently spatial aspects of its subject. Only consider the actual course (notice the spatial allusion!) of any of the ceremonies mentioned,

discern of just what it consists and its profoundly spatial character becomes salient.

Any considerable ritual must presuppose correct surroundings; validity depends upon a proper venue. Simple location itself does not alone
define the venue. Internal layout as well is essential, establishing a ceremonious routing across a number of formalized boundaries. It leads the
individual in passage through a prescribed itinerary, from one station to
another, each tenanted by a specific officiant. At each minor threshold,
an obeisance or similarly supplicating display is exacted from the candidate crossing. Appropriate costumes, decor, and declamations lend authenticity and gravity to the proceedings. If this skeleton description
summons up images of high school commencements, marriage ceremonies, funeral processions, war dances, pilgrimages to Mecca, or military
truce negotiations, it has made its point. But let it also stand, in a much
less grandiose way, to be sure, for ordinary, everyday behavior.

Action in and through an institution obeys the same format, essentially, as that just described for any rite of passage, grandiose or minute.
It can therefore be inferred that the institution's interior spaces will be
configured or laid out in such a way as to accommodate whatever itineraries its ceremonies entail. (Just picture a courtroom, a mosque, a parade ground, an American Indian dance house.) Moreover, the resulting
differentiation applies to the personnel concerned, as well, with a system
of social distinctions as its normal result.

Institutions conduct rites of passage, if mostly exceedingly minor
ones. As all the foregoing intimates, a major part of an institution's business revolves around transformations of identity or status of both its own
integral members and other people subject to its ministrations. This generalization applies as much to what goes on in a retail shop as to supreme
court deliberations: the window-shopper, "Just looking, thank you," is
transmuted into a proprietor of some object through the act of presenting the clerk with a credit card, for instance, thereby converting the
issuer of the card into the buyer's creditor. In this way, the transaction
establishes new social relationships.

In fact nothing, other than the fact that somewhat more imposing
established institutions (such as churches or government offices) normally solemnize them, distinguishes van Gennep's grand rites of passage
from the homelier ones of everyday life.

The ceremoniality and operating principles that institutional members impart through example and instruction to initiates—the tradition
or institutional culture—persist over time, although not without modi-

fication, such as happens in any process of diffusion. Tradition and attributed history, rehearsed and elaborated in concrete, public words and deeds, endow an institution with its own historical career and "personality," which live on only in the sometimes faulty repetition of similar words and deeds. Equally, however, physical concreteness lends institutions a particular spatial identity and a relatively solid and durable one, which is what most concerns us here. Distinctive physical, spatial properties tend to manifest themselves in institutions generally.

The endless succession of small transactions that figure in and facilitate everyone's humble itineraries also have their properly differentiated venues and appropriate displays. The foregoing account refers to the venue of major ritual action—its spatial layout, material content, and verbal performances, incidental to the procession through it. Those material components reinforce each other's function mutually and tend of themselves to fix and regularize proceedings within, both in the case of the grander life-transitions and in that of the daily spatial routine. In particular, explicitly constructed containers, as Lewis Mumford called them, such as buildings and other enclosures must, in addition to their role of exclusion, perforce permit passage inward as well as outward and therefore, when defended or monitored at all, funnel movement toward points of significant encounter. Every castle has to have gates in its walls, however well guarded.

A castle represents considerably more than just a private home. It houses activities and personnel that serve an external constituency. It also protects them, and for this reason exemplifies another condition resembling true territoriality, and ultimately deriving perhaps from defense of home places, but clearly secondary to a primary mosaic-and-network spatial complex. Elevated to another level, so to speak, it can discharge broader societal functions. Good grounds exist, including purely historical ones, for considering the castle and its more primitive prototypes good instances of secondary territoriality, as an archetypical and distinctively human invention.

Conforming to a tendency widespread in the living world, human beings almost everywhere have long constructed, or sometimes just commandeered, protected dwelling places. The basic merit of construction (or of any refuge) is certainly not simply that it absolutely obstructs all in-and-out traffic (of course it must not), but rather that, providing apertures for entry and exit, at the same time it concentrates control at one or a few critical and advantageously defensible points in the enclosure.

Among animals this ordinarily means the rigid exclusion not only of alien creatures but also of all fellow members of the species except those of the resident breeding unit, despite the fact that conspecifics not closely related may meet freely in foraging ranges. In this respect, human hospitality to other humans is something unusual. Mechanisms of conciliation, such as those discussed earlier in this chapter, afford through ceremoniality the means of converting unacceptable identities into welcome ones.

This peculiar human attribute, enabling outsiders to commingle with residents despite the latter's protective structures and guarded entrances, permits far more than simply friendly visiting. It creates, for one thing, expanded opportunities to engage in mutual learning and influence and, for another, propitious conditions for working together. Its greatest benefit may consist in making possible the secondary territoriality just mentioned.

Circumscribed, defended sites of congregation and joint enterprise, of which the ancient castle and perhaps related temple (cf. Wheatley, 1971) probably can stand as prototypes, owe their existence entirely to the suspension of the more primitive, or primary, type of territoriality expressed in automatic home defense reactions. Not that such secondary sites remain undefended; quite the contrary, they characteristically exhibit redoubtable fortifications.

However, their crucial utility stems from the fact that access to them is open, although on a decidedly selective basis, to a large and heterogeneous population, thanks again to statuses conferred by major and minor rites of passage. Common enterprise can then draw on an extensive pool of talents and energies, while the secondary territorial defense shelters their activities from interference. Their contingent exclusivity plays an indispensable role in fostering social integration but, as will be shown, likewise inevitably concentrates and insulates political (and hence social and economic) power, frequently to the detriment of most of the community. What I here call castles contain the precincts of power that, in Chapter 11, will be discussed under the rubric of "smoke-filled rooms."

Congregation and collaboration throve within the selective and protective exclusivity of the medieval castle but prosper just as well within such kindred, commonplace enclosures as the factory and office building, the temple and bazaar. Indeed it is likely, as Wheatley suggests, that all the varied functions now housed in these multifarious constructions once, in ancient times, were concentrated in the castle itself. The castle had its own granaries and workshops; modern warehouses and factories descend from them. The dungeon and the guardroom have become the jail and midcity garrison. The throne room turned into the courthouse and the warrens of bureaucracy.

This universe of secondary territoriality is par excellence the universe of institutions. Its most fundamental components consist of associated groups of living people, without whom institutions evaporate into mere names, for institutions are only enacted. The defining feature of each is the distinctive practices in which its members regularly engage. So the term "institution" refers to both actors and action, as well as simply to castle-like place. The regularity of the characteristic action, that is, the institution's ceremoniality, calls for appropriate venues, which fact indicates its usual propensity toward incorporation in an edifice expressly selected and equipped for its uses. As with actual castles, the diverse and imposing forms these constructions may take often proudly proclaim their particular functions, and thereby dignify a landscape.

Confined spaces like castles not only inhibit free access of unwanted parties, but also, precisely by virtue of this, they ensure to those admitted within them freedom from disturbance, essential to working and communicating safely and comfortably. Their role in protecting and nourishing the social collaboration of people, albeit by no means always impartially or even judiciously, helps both to manage modification of natural surroundings and to alter the standings of people. Here, too, rites of passage are prone to be enacted, and here as well sit the centers or subcenters of the major networks diffusing imitative behavior routines.

Not merely do human beings themselves get around, among "castles" as well as at large. In addition, much of what they utter as display also can potentially circulate widely. And even the objects they manufacture are extensively dispersed in the process of trade. The ensuing chapter details the diffusion mechanisms involved.

NINE

• Spread the Word

"Word gets around . . ." What could say it any better? That is the point of diffusion, when all display is included. The term has been used in various ways. "Gaseous diffusion" (having nothing at all to do with talk, let us hope!) is described in physical terms by Graham's Law. In the atmosphere, the diffusion of incoming sunlight affects the earth's energy budget. Many writers have discussed the diffusion of gossip, ideas, innovations, inventions, and culture. This chapter will deal with the latter phenomena, the driving mechanism of cultural development and change, an effect of personal Geltung.

Communication must, after all, consist of the transmission of signs, signals, or stimuli, that is, of uttered displays, over some distance, minute though it often be. Even a heart-to-heart talk would qualify, albeit what part the actual heart may be playing is moot. It makes perfectly good sense to suppose that the process begins when one transmitter—in this case, either an animal or a human, equipped if required with some gadgetry—reaches some receiver, over no matter what channel. And much of diffusion stops there, in the primary act of display. But if a reply ensues and the receiver repeats more or less the initial behavior, the impulse may be propagated repeatedly and generate a broader "diffusion field" in space or in time or in both. A path-breaking book by one of the greatest geographers ever, Torsten Hägerstrand (1967), has inspired a large volume of recent work on this process.

Personal Geltung attaching to agents involved in transmission furnishes the switching mechanism that determines the flow. The Geltung potential in matter received, as assessed by recipients, governs retention and often further transmission.

A distinction ought to be drawn between what takes place within a single dyad, between just two partners, and what happens when that initial exchange plugs into other circuits, that is, when Geltung or some other factor impels one or both of the initial partners to retransmit the impulse in subsequent dyadic exchange with different interlocutors, and this expansive linking and repetition goes on for a while. Then we can really speak of diffusion.

This characterization of diffusion takes us back to imitative learning, of course. In fact, the retention of an activity pattern, be it merely the ability to repeat a phrase, is crucial to any diffusion, although, as will shortly be shown, the repetition involved may not be quite accurate. And of course in time the learning may fade.

Diffusion processes of the sort described are ubiquitous and indeed virtually infinite in number and variety. They insert themselves, like nerve impulses in a body, into almost all human doings, and most of them pass without notice. Every time we begin with, "They say . . . ," or inquire, "Who told you that?" or "Where did you ever get such an idea?" we are supposing diffusion.

Each step in any diffusion of an innovation and therefore all that transpires in the overall process conform to the same dyadic interaction format already depicted: a series of repeated provocations and all that they entail. In accordance with the principle of freedom, each is theoretically unpredictable; and each falls subject to demands, potentially, for external, independent, real world confirmation.

At every step, too, the Geltung effect becomes evident. People heed best the displays of others whose Geltung impresses them, and imitate best the displays that appear to yield Geltung to them, often confirmed by some sort of testing.

Furthermore, no doubt every utterance involved in a diffusion must retain and suffer from a bit of ineluctable inscrutability. Everything said or shown, in order to provoke, must be just a bit of a puzzle; for just as the concept of information requires that any response must be open and free, within the constraints of the format, so the supposed "meaning" of a provocative utterance will possibly remain somewhat unfathomable to an interlocutor. We often have to ask, "Is this what you wanted?" "Is that what you meant?" What ethnologists call "stimulus diffusion" will provide a good instance of this latter principle.

In many parts of the world, the so-called natives (we are all natives, though, aren't we?) have been observed to take up Western social usages and the use of Western artifacts, in quite unexpected ways. I particularly like the good Japanese word, *waishatsu*, referring to any men's shirt, whatever its hue; it comes from "white shirt." Or take the Russian word for a railway station, *vokzal*, derived from the name of London's Vauxhall Station. Languages abound with such cockeyed borrowings, and so do other cultural features, learned by imitation, indeed, but not quite according to the original prescription.

Take modern plumbing fixtures as another example. They diffused out of northwestern Europe rather briskly. But in the process they went, so to speak, from sit to squat, accommodating the older habits of the receiving populations. When the late Ayatollah Khomeini established his headquarters near Paris, it is reported, his retinue ripped out the Western toilets installed in the local houses they took over and replaced them with the perilous porcelain pits that prevail in Iran, as well for example as in Japan.

Gossip gives the most familiar case: when a story spreads, it always changes and eventually becomes distorted and almost unrecognizable; examples abound.

Not only do alleged messages get misread and miscast, but they also run into plenty of competition. In a world where everybody is talking and gesturing and showing off things all at once, a plethora of intersecting, interfering impulses swarm out of infinitely varied sources and tend to swamp receivers: information overload is nothing new. The very spatiotemporal pattern of diffused communication, a centrifugal one unless modified, guarantees that some, at least, of all the output will proliferate. Impulses may fan out in all directions from initiators. No wave length is protected, no broadcast area (notice, incidentally, that we are all in this sense broadcasters) is kept free of crowding, clashing stations. Diffusion processes go on constantly from and toward every direction, arising in multiple sources and following various channels. Unique sources of culture are simply not credible. Europe has certainly not been the source of all good things, or all good people (cf. Blaut, 1993).

Our youth, that intriguing mystery, is clearly perplexed, in Western countries and now increasingly elsewhere, by all this confusion. Young people have to navigate many incompatible diffusion fields at once, multiply centered on the home and family, the school, the crowd around the drive-in restaurant, the rock extravaganza, the place where they work to support indispensable cars, the TV and videos, the shopping center. Their sometimes distant drummers have their own beat. Whereas their elders may attune to fewer sources of communication and be better off for it, the young are subjected, as never before, to a painfully discordant chorus of images and exhortations. Similarly confusing waves of information also tend to assail people living in so-called traditional cultures. Little wonder that a distressingly ragged society and a wretched Third World result.

To be sure, all societies are almost by definition more or less traditional, or they simply would not exist. It is really inappropriate to contrast traditional and modern, for every society that exists now (or whenever) is both, in its time. This undoubted fact of ubiquitous tradition signifies that "not everything goes"; all societies award clear preference only to certain ways of behaving and attend only to certain informants, exemplars, mentors, and authorities, that is, to those with the most Geltung. At a finer scale families, religious groups, and the educational establishment attempt likewise to harness and monopolize the flows of information. Thus they and countless other institutions all attempt in their fashion to domesticate diffusion and abate confusion and conflict. "When in Rome, do as the Romans do" was surely a rule requiring enforcement.

Every dog has its day, and every person alive will have his or her word. We each have some tale worth the telling, as also do some of the dead. Every scrap of what is diffused in communication begins somewhere with one person, with what somebody says or somebody does. One by one, also, individuals must choose to accept it in order to set a diffusion in motion.

If you want to understand people, watch babies. Tiny infants react in an "animal" way in the face of their surroundings, searching and experimenting, then recoiling from repellent stimuli and going on to sample more of attractive ones. If something attracts them they reach after it or even try to put it into their mouths; if another object alarms them, they scream bloody murder. That exhibition of stimulus and response alone reveals much about human behavior more generally.

A telling example of diffusion in operation likewise occurs even before a child learns to speak. Notice that people call "baby talk" not what the infant is uttering so much as the attempts of adults to imitate it. The baby's gurgles and mouthings diffuse to its caretakers! This observable fact also shows that every newborn human being begins to invent right away, and goes on doing so all its life. In fact, despite all the trial-and-error learning, an individual probably retains this facility and early invents and lifelong employs a very slightly different way of speaking than any other human does. Everyone speaks in an idiolect, a somewhat un-stable, idiosyncratic, personal (but as Wittgenstein pointed out, not re-ally private) language. Imperfect as copiers, individuals invent their own language, just a shade unlike anyone else's, in trying to imitate speech that they hear.

Diffusion, too, starts with invention. How many times has the wheel been invented? There is no way of knowing for sure, but it may be supposed that the principle has been discovered countless times in the past. Yet it would seldom have diffused successfully, and so time and again it would die with its finder and be lost again for a while. The pre-Columbian civilizations of the New World provide exactly such a case. The Olmecs, Mayas, Incas, Aztecs, and other ingenious peoples in this hemisphere achieved remarkable technical feats in many domains, but they apparently failed or neglected to harness the wheel to practical uses. Some quaint toys unearthed in Mexico bear witness to awareness of the wheel principle, but no evidence exists to suggest that it was widely applied, or even that the making of wheeled toys continued for long. An invention, yes, but not of much consequence, since it progressed no further than the toymaker's shop.

As Joseph Needham (1985) has demonstrated so well, the imaginative, industrious Chinese, too, deserve credit for many important inven-tions—important, at least, to us now—upon which they declined to capitalize: among them, the compass, gunpowder, block printing, paper money, coal used for fuel, and so on. The Greeks even had a modest steam engine that they never saw fit to propel a ship with.

Influential invention requires not merely someone's discovering or devising something new, but showing it and then its adoption by others. The diffusion that follows may or may not go as far as it might, as the Chinese and Mexican examples illustrate. We can formulate the stages either of invention in particular or of diffused information in general as follows: inspiration, perhaps preceded by observational or imitative learning; perspiration (trial-and-error experimentation); demonstration (display); adoption (imitative learning); and then repeated display and possibly further adoptions. Personal Geltung assuredly plays a large role in this process.

The sequence followed is the same for slang words or campaign slo-gans as it is for junk foods or jogging shoes. In other words, every diffu-sion has roots in invention. This invokes freedom again: a person's re-sponse to the challenge or provocations of any experience, discourse or otherwise, is always up to that person. So what is done with a hint of, or insight into, nature's behavior is as much up to the individual adapter or inventor as response to a question would be. Likewise, the principle of interchangeability comes into play here once again: for instance, verbal consultation (of colleagues or of published precedent) may go along with experimental activity, in science or otherwise, to expedite research and creation, and both description and demonstration of results may foster adoption and therefore diffusion.

Many culture historians debate the alternatives of what they call "independent invention" or diffusion. The formulation just proposed would appear to obviate the choice. All diffusion starts with inventions, and all inventions must diffuse in order to count for something. The issue really seems to hang on the contrast between unique inventions, restricted to a single time and place and never repeated or duplicated elsewhere yet somehow widely diffused, and inventions that occur more than once in separate centers and then diffuse for some distance.

Communication likewise favors further invention. Much useful innovation consists in "putting two and two together," that is, discerning and realizing potential new fusions of principles already known. Consider a ridiculous illustration: A story tells of a monument erected in a small town in China honoring the inventor of the chopstick. In the next little town another monument commemorates the person who developed the second chopstick. This absurdity proclaims the importance of recombination in the process of invention. The greater the stock of existing, adopted inventions and insights, the greater will be the expectable number of their possible permutations and combinations, ready to prompt creativity. Cultural richness, artistic and linguistic as much as strictly technological, should increase in direct proportion both to the backlog of what has been learned beforehand and to the briskness and density of prevailing communication. In this regard, as in others, the spatial aspects of diffusion systems are of prime importance. Consider them now.

A good deal of diffusion occurs in casual contexts and covers a limited area. But since institutions, so stodgy and uninventive in their repetitious rituality, nonetheless link numerous people together and engage extensively in communication, they play an increasingly dominant role in long-distance diffusion.

Types of institutions abound, and each has its own agenda and audience to which it diffuses information. They overlap and interfere with each other. This makes for uneasy complexity and often for trouble.

Institutions live lives, in space and in time; more precisely, the people whose actions alone constitute and continue an institution's existence live their lives embroiled in institutional, interactional relationships enacted in space and time. The spatial manifestation of the institution's clientele is best portrayed as a loose constellation of scattered points in space.

Visualize a television station and its audience as spatial entities. The zone within reach of the broadcaster's signals consists, first of all, of a fairly unbroken patchwork ("mosaic") of homes, each cozily discrete. The premises occupied by the station (secondary territories analogous to a "castle") figure not as sectors of a continuous patchwork but rather as parts of a polka dot pattern, spotted here and there with the seats of many different sorts of institutions. Between the studios themselves, the transmitters and towers, the business and accounting offices, the advertising division, the trucks and crews on location, the possibly distant corporate headquarters, and still other components of the station run lines of fixed or intermittent connection, forming a network.

When a particular program is broadcast, some but not all of the homes within the mosaic tune in. Represent the resulting audience again as a spatial array of points. It will consist of a ragged, unevenly dense distribution, probably fading away around the edges and registering here and there, as clots and gaps within it, the demographic variables that index viewer preferences. It resembles the heavens at night, justifying the name constellation.

The implications of this spatial modeling become more vivid if you suppose that some of the homes in the impact area house a number of family members of both genders and various ages. Then you may imagine that several TV sets flicker and blare simultaneously in different rooms. While father watches, say, a football game, the youngest kids are transfixed by *Sesame Street*, mother picks up some new recipes, and the teens undergo a rock video. There's something for everyone. The family is apportioned among the different constellations generated by the respective, and often pathetically respectful, viewers of each of the various broadcasting networks invading the house, based perhaps in different cities.

Family life attempts to proceed harmoniously amid all the disparate, often conflicting, displays and instigations flooding into the home. If you will now expand the list of impinging constellations to embrace those of schools, churches, clubs, workplaces, kinship, sporting teams, motion pictures, newspapers, radio, billboards, and any other diffusion media you can think of, you can appreciate the complexity of modern communication in the technically most advanced countries. That same competitive multiplicity of appeals impinges not only on bona fide families but as well, for instance, on the large proportion of Americans and Canadians who live outside regular families.

The case was far simpler only a few decades ago, of course, and in many societies around the world it remains so still. Yet even a remote island, or a mountain village in a poor country, harbors a plurality of such constellations and networks. Religious cults, secret societies, age sets, market confederations, warrior bands, political movements, clans, castes, or classes, and maybe a handful of missionaries and rural police fraction even most of what are somewhat improperly called "primitive" societies. And few such communities enjoy full autonomy or relax in complete isolation, so that they too have to contend with influences ultimately diffusing from the larger world.

What, then, can possibly glue a society together and keep it united enough to still function?

Offhand, it might be supposed that consensus could somehow be enforced through prohibition of unauthorized novelties. There are maxims to guard against knowing too much that is too different from the common wisdom: "Ignorance is bliss"; "What you don't know won't hurt you"; and, less radical, "You mustn't believe everything you hear." The complacency expressed may be distasteful, but such injunctions do serve as operational rules in every cultural community. They seek to countervail against overwhelming, discordant diffusion. Unfortunately, as has just been illustrated, a multiplicity of institutions still are usually competing to get their different images and exhortations across, provoking incompatible reactions among a populace.

Far more potent than maxims are institutional practices that centralize, channel, and more or less standardize decision and diffusion. They have been depicted in Chapter 8 partly under the rubric of "rites of passage," specifically the grander established, collective ceremonials, such as those of law, religion, and administration. Some of them are mandatory for entire regional populations, whereas others still reveal themselves in spotty constellations of adherents or clients. Commonly, institutions encharged with such regulative functions claim and enforce primacy over less formalized, stable, or enduring sources of diffusion.

Just as an army tries to seize territory from its enemy in order to impose its government's rule, through dominant diffusion, on the resident population (and resources), institutions of communication attempt to incorporate actual spatial domains, whether networks or constellations, into their spheres of jurisdiction. They employ an explicit strategy of spatial consolidation, analogous to that of an empire. In fact, many an empire has stood as a grand example of this strategy, and left behind imposing traces of its former preponderance in language, law, religion, custom, and, obviously, art and architecture.

The institutional organization and communicative processes within an area may have progressed over time from an imaginable mosaic of isolated, autonomous home territories, animal-style, attuned only to internal and immediately peripheral display, through successive unifying steps. But that pristine stage when exclusive human territoriality may have prevailed vanished long ago. Societies do not live that way, and humans are entirely social and, conditionally, spatially open. Gradually, emerging networks of communication and control have condensed societies as entities. Diffusion creates and compacts cultural realms and political regions. In part the limits of these spatial units become set by human endeavor, but as always environmental barriers can inhibit indefinite expansion.

Internal differentiation proceeding among the populations of such cultural regions has fostered the creation of varied collections of institutions. The latter establish their centers in "castle" sites of secondary territoriality, out of which radiate networks connecting their outposts. Those substations serve to communicate with the population, either to broadcast directly to whatever constellation of clients they can attract or else to conduct institutional business within their own precincts as rites of passage. The multiple networks thread through the region and conjointly diffuse what becomes the distinctive stuff of the culture. They afford a kind of curriculum for imitative learning.

However, you can lead a horse to water, but you can't make it drink. The populace may resist or remain indifferent and not soak up the flood of informational provocations gushing out of the networks. In order to achieve even a partial monopoly of diffusion, the institutions concerned must also set off a further repetitive circulation of communicative impulses, operating through everyday face-to-face encounters. When contrary waves of diffusion, of which the so-called counterculture in North America was a good example, somehow prevail, the institutional impetus can be swamped and neutralized.

The much deplored American school situation may exemplify this frustrating phenomenon. Educational institutions attempt to propagate certain models and methods of behavior. They have to contend, however, with defiant and even derisive reactions not only from pupils enmeshed in alternative networks exalting truancy, cars, rock music, and dope, but also from skeptical, unsupportive, unlettered parents; pinch-penny schoolboards and governments; snooping community censors; and yet other competitors. Not only schools try to educate, and at times the schools scarcely can.

The churches and temples face a like challenge. Entranced with alternative excitements, such as sports and weekend excursions, and no longer impressed perhaps with eternity, people find different uses for Sabbath.

Again, commercial advertisers must work very hard to hold on to their audience. This requires a constant, imaginative titillation of the target populace. The displays employed must dangle before the audience the sorts of arousing images that get through to it. If you want to sell beer, don't talk about beer; talk about bustlines and ball games. The brewing companies have become the major Maecenases of the implausible arts of sport, thus tapping into popular networks of diffusion and courting participants' patronage. Similarly, anorexic models slink before a fashion-hungry female audience in order to entice much bulkier, dowdier customers into buying the product.

In the final analysis, successful mass communication depends on reaching and activating whole masses of people in their own terms. *Vox populi, vox Dei.* Great, anonymous, and commonplace diffusion fields affecting everyone constantly grow out of and come to transcend those of institutions. Although the term "mass communication" is rather a misnomer (it remains always only dyadic!), the advantages of suffusing masses of people with congenial images are quite understandable.

In order to produce much effect, the institutional impulse diffused, the "message," has to spread beyond just the initial receiver; it would cost far too much to convince each client, customer, or convert, one by one. An institution needs to establish a sort of spreading consensus that prevails beyond its own reach in order to make its pitch for popularity. The message takes a free ride on the discourse of subsequent dyads that carry it onward. Casual chatter comes into its own as diffusion when repeating the institutional message. Advertisers long most for word-of-mouth support.

An institution must not only enlist the aid of word-of-mouth transmission by its initiates, however. It as well has to either conform to or counter the control inflicted by the commentary and criticism that circulate unceasingly within a community and all its component dyads. The actions learned from its broadcasts or proceedings and repeated be-

fore interlocutors undergo sharp scrutiny and screening within immediate, intimate contexts of firsthand personal interaction. Parents quiz
kids about both their schoolwork and their leisure-time habits. Women
attentive to Geltung may mercilessly assess their peers' hairdos and
makeup. Males often screen their associates by "macho" criteria.

How handy might be a diagram that could show the multifarious
pairings (still dyads) that perform the communicative work of autonomous discourse! It would have to reveal the routes over lines of connection, both public and proprietary, that carry the traffic of all sorts of
business. In a technically advanced system, those routes become so numerous as to defy description. At issue, though, are not simply the great
abundance of varied physical conduits available, frequently flexibly
combinable, ranging from meetings and messengers to instant facsimile
facilities and computer modems. Far more important yet are the actual
pathways picked out over any of the many optional, combinational rout-
ings that may be selected.

On top of all that, so much goes on all at once that any attempt at a
static portrayal would soon produce such an overcrowded graph that its
sense would be obliterated. At every instant the system totally metamor-
phoses. Countless transmissions are constantly being activated or extin-
guished. Any given connection only functions ephemerally. So, as usual,
space without time tells us little.

The spatial pattern of a universe of disjoint, scattered inventors or
simply communicators lends itself to visualization, again, as a constellation, precisely analogous to that described for the impact zone of broadcast displays, except for its reverse direction of impulses. It will comprise
an irregular array of points at varying densities, each of them the momentary locus of a communicative event (according to the preceding
interpretation of invention). If it pictured the heavens it might blink like
the stars, and, indeed, a twinkling picture should best convey the on-
and-off nature of the events of innovation under discussion, and aid in
tracking them over time.

Watch one tiny, particular spot, which comes alight to represent a free
and active individual emitting a signal, displaying. After a moment, while
the first signal shines, some surrounding points may illuminate in turn,
and as time goes on an expanding concentric wave of light will surge
forth. Probably the field is not filled by a solid, ever-growing disk of
brightness; it should look more like a brilliant explosion of fireworks
into night skies, with streamers flailing out in all directions and darkness
between. Not every point reached by the impulse makes a response. On

occasion, the whole visible field will indeed become suffused with light after a time, although often this fails to occur.

Somewhere actual displays reach physical limits, and so likewise may the actual diffusion field. Topographical barriers halt or impede diffusion so often that cultural boundaries frequently, strikingly, mirror them. Or linguistic or cultural incomprehension may set similar bounds to diffusion. If what one's neighbor says is gibberish, one can learn little from it. Thus the available diffusion field, at any given instant, is not infinite.

We have a disheartening saying that goes, "Out of sight, out of mind." Although the poet who pines for some lover may find consolation in the opposite adage, "Absence makes the heart grow fonder," the reality is notoriously often otherwise. The former phrase embodies a notion of which geographers are fond, rather impalatably referred to as "time-distance decay." What it signifies here is that as the impulse travels onward the little lights in our model will flicker and fade out, and that fewer and fewer responses will occur as the wave proceeds. Initial inputs of Geltung may weaken and not be renewed. The farther away and the longer ago something happened, the less its effect here and now. The so-called decay of an impulse really consists of a gradual decrease over distance and time in the frequency of its acceptance and retransmission, and therefore implies dilution of its relative influence.

The amount of so-called decay must bear some relation to the comparative potency of any original impulse. A very strong surge will last longer and spread out more widely, other things being equal. Furthermore, a close concentration of numerous individuals emitting similar impulses increases the chances for widespread diffusion. The potency of such a net impulse is approximately a function of population size, that is, of the mass of potential communicators at the point or in the place emitting the initial signal. For example, the number of individuals inhabiting a given city gives a clue to how far away they might find mates. It can be reliably predicted that more New Yorkers will marry people from Iowa than will the same number of Alaskans. "In numbers is strength"—or cornfed romance.

But then Chicago comes into the picture. Although less populous than New York, Chicago, being closer to Iowa, will enjoy an advantage of its own and probably capture more Iowan spouses than even the Big Apple does. The two factors play off against each other. Geographers and sociologists call this second effect intervening opportunity. It can present itself as a very real influence in cases where competing diffusion fields of varied potencies operate. Intervening opportunities tempt children to play hooky; a gang of truant companions is often more potently persuasive than a schoolteacher.

The crude model just proposed lacks finesse and needs to be complemented by subtler ones that account for the communicative roles of institutions, their premises, their networks and domains, and of course the anonymous casual babble of everyone in particular. By and large, however, an impulse passing over an institutional network should follow the same progression outward from its initiator along the branches of the network and be subject to the same interruptions and impediments.

The difference between diffusion over networks and that across an unconfigured field looks almost illusory; the latter merely uncovers a latent network of congenial receivers, perhaps preconditioned by earlier contacts. "Success feeds on success," and the prospect that a receiver will adopt the next impulse or display from any given interlocutor should probably vary nearly in proportion to the quantum of antecedent adoptions from that source. In other words, you pay attention to people you know and respect, who have Geltung.

Failing such firsthand inducements, people lend their attention and credence to given organized systems of regular interaction—institutions, again. We go on next to reflect on certain decisive effects of an individual's placement within or relative to such established social and spatial communicative complexes.

Working Together •

"**Y**ou've gotta get with the system," we say, and with reason. Our very survival depends on submergence in systems—communicative systems constantly regulating Geltung and spatial arrangements.

Living humanity in its entirety, along with some deceased predecessors and including some artifacts, should hypothetically constitute a global communication system; information slowly diffuses through it. Behavioral "mutations," inventions, small variations and combinations of acts, may become accepted and spread. At the other extreme, each dyadic communication between two partners itself briefly constitutes a separate system, made up of its momentarily unique spatial arrangement, venue, and procedure. The enactment of institutional rites of passage avails itself of a formalized system of spatial relationships allied with prescribed performance formulas and suitable items of pomp to constitute another sort of system. Certainly an institutional network also evinces this character, as do broadcast agencies together with their constellated audiences.

"Everything seems to be going 'round and 'round" describes how communication works: in circuits. The section just previous to this chapter referred to diffusion conveyed by technical means. It featured especially networks and constellations, always insisting on the dyadic principle and hence the reciprocity of information flows in both structures: give and take, 'round and 'round. It construed broadcast diffusion as the activation of multiple individual dyads, each linked back to the broadcaster via some simple or elaborately complex closing circuit.

This chapter will describe some much more elaborated patterns of diffusion, in which numerous pairings of people, abetted at times by artificial devices, join together as discrete and integrated systems.

Within a system, change in one constituent element triggers change in other involved elements, but not necessarily outside the system. This principle underlies all social and technical organization, as well as much else in nature.

Systematic connections and progressions coordinate and differentiate individual human activities in space and time. The concerted joint effort permitted by them empowers humanity to achieve what no other known species has done on anything like a comparable scale. Human learning, for instance, ascends to new potentialities when example, practice, and coaching are systematized, and hence it can make efficient use of the capacity to benefit lifelong from imitation. The learner not merely observes, but is shown; the teacher not only acts, but also exemplifies.

Formal institutions of learning illustrate how an established system of communicative interactions, emplaced within suitable precincts and properly equipped with accessory tools, accomplishes its tasks. The North American school system, a good epitome, is compounded of a large array of varied elements conjoined. The list for just one primary school includes its physical plant, consisting of classrooms and offices; recreational, sanitary, health, and food service facilities; its equipment, such as textbooks and teaching materials; its teachers and pupils, administrators, janitors, nurses, and various other personnel; the procedural provisions of its budget, curriculum, disciplinary rules, and schedules; the school board looming above it; the parent association. Under its instituted procedures, within the school's physical setting and employing equipment provided, a multitude of dyadic interactions among personnel, and with objects, go on constantly. All of them ideally serve the sovereign purpose of classroom dialog and learning. Every element mentioned is subject to effects produced by the behavior of any other. And despite all the hazards, some learning results.

What kind of diagram could fairly represent such a school? No less will do than a veritable labyrinth of sporadic, dyadic linkage loops— principal and teacher, pupil and pupil, parent and school nurse, janitor and assistant principal, teacher and member of class, and every conceivable permutation—that will be strewn, or stretched by telephone, across the physical plant, enhanced by objects invoked.

Probably the majority of institutions do generate similar tangles of one sort or another. An ordinary factory will, for example. But likewise a factory may feature within its total system a production line, actually something more interesting than a simple line, which exemplifies another distinct spatial pattern and therefore a peculiar communicative situation.

Like Old Man River, a production line "just keeps movin' along." It resembles a river as well in receiving tributary flows from time to time and finally ending in something recalling the deltaic distributaries of a big stream. But whereas a watercourse is interrupted by myriad rapids and dams, the flow of stuff in production, although it can roll onward as smoothly as water, encounters a series of critical control points along its way. At each such phase-station in the industrial progression, operatives intervene to summon inputs of energy, externally manufactured components, and raw materials from tributary sources or to effect combinations and transformations of materials (cf. Wagner, 1960). The stream can move forward only when requisite work is accomplished at each given station. Unlike that of many heavily diverted rivers today, however, the volume of flow in industrial plants need not decrease at each phase. On the contrary, something is constantly being added, under the control of workers operating their machines.

The detailed map of a river system will do as a model for the diagram of any production line and, imagined as "telescoped" down into one point, will also represent other spatiotemporal layouts of production. The gross features consist of the stream and its incoming tributaries and, commonly then, at its mouth, distributaries fanning out in a delta. Where do the workers at their stations figure in the image, though? Well, to carry the analogy further, suppose that snags and stumps and big rocks in the river, around which activity swirls, can represent the individual working positions, appearing aligned along the whole course of the stream. What shall we call it—a "potamic structure"? You may prefer to imagine a strictly dendritic diagram, for a tree, after all, is nothing more than a wooden-banked river that flows in reverse toward the sky. But imagine the flow running downward, as rainwater does in the forest.

Such a "step-by-step" image of industrial production lines illustrates the fundamental principles common to so-called batch as well as flow processes, despite the concentration of the former in one spot, and in fact applies to any sequential production, even in agriculture. All depend on a systematization of operations depending on a ruling spatiotemporal order. Furthermore, they all reflect the division of labor dear to economists, expressed in space and time as well as in task. In this

system, "there's a time and a place for everything," and someone qualified must be on hand at each phase to do whatever is required then and
there.

Nowadays the flows, and comparable sequences in batch and all other
organized production, are mostly propelled by inanimate power. Yet
what actually keeps them in motion can be recognized as communication. "Just give the word," and action begins. That cue triggers the single
initiating action, but under a production scheme the completion of each
phase constitutes a signal to proceed to the next. More often than not,
the rates and rhythms of work, however, obey more-comprehensive
directives imposed from above as well.

Although most of the cues may present themselves automatically as
processing moves along, they are after all provocations to act and can
hence be assimilated into a communication model. In the aggregate,
they constitute a sequence of miniscule episodes of dyadic provocation
and response displays, ordinarily expressed in the media of objects and
actions rather than words, but still expressly communicative. Those are
what keep things moving.

Placement within a processive order akin to the kinds just described,
and in fact into other sorts too, profoundly affects an individual's status
and Geltung. Where particular people fit into a production line, a school
system, or any other spatial arrangement, tends to mark their identity
and some of their options in life.

The Japanese language accords explicit recognition to a salient relationship between occupation and location, for instance designating both
a seafood seller's shop and the actual fishmonger with a single word, "*sa-
kanaya.*" In polite address, it respectfully calls the merchant "*sakanaya-
san*"—Madame or Mister Fish Store. Thus Japanese treats place, work,
and person as one. This usage points up the close correspondence among
the spatial, the technical, and the social—indeed, the personal—aspects
of labor. Thus, understandably, resentful industrial workers complain on
occasion that they feel like "only cogs in a machine."

Within the production system, position keeps people "doing their
thing." Every station on the line, or operation in batch work, or role in
the teaching and learning endeavor awaits the (communicative) initiative
of the just preceding operative: that governs the rhythm and also the
nature of a given worker's action. Where you stand tells what you may
do, and maybe even partly who you can be. The layout of productive
apparatus in a factory itself ordains, simply by spatial means, important
relationships and roles. More broadly, perhaps nearly always, as most of
the foregoing discussion implies, place has much to do with one's fate.

In somewhat wider context than the shop floor, a job in some particular factory, or office (much the same), or department store defines a horizon of possible action, and even perhaps the norms of deportment in general. It can go so far as to govern habitual association and friendships to some extent, tending to create "birds of a feather" through casual diffusion. This observation applies to activities throughout the domain of any society. Propinquity favors affinity.

The overall communicative matrix of production is comprised of many more sorts of dyads than those treated above, to be sure. Regarding labor as dialog, we discern that the time a worker spends on the line, whether busy or not, discharges a second essential communicative role, often registered by punching the time clock and in getting a paycheck. All the planning, administrative, engineering, payroll, and supervisory initiatives that regulate production also consist of complexes of dyadic interactions, very much as in the school example examined above. Then there are transactions with the world beyond. Those negotiate, among other things, the inputs of energy, materials, and possibly specialized technical advice to the process and also determine the destination of outputs. A proper depiction of this management matrix, too, would dictate another tangle of dyads.

The foregoing remarks ought clearly to intimate that all of everyday business consists of diffusions of at least minutely innovative information. Directives, reports, and other performances that travel back and forth in an office or factory, military orders and their execution, proceedings at law, liturgical intonations and congregational responses, lessons taught and recited in class, conversations: all of these and many other kinds of exchanges transmit and hence at least briefly diffuse information, and often it propagates widely. The picture given of productive enterprise is in fact a universal picture of everyday life and communication.

However, the foregoing are not the only portraits we can paint of enterprise. It packs many parts into composite wholes at various levels. For instance, markets exist within markets; markets incorporate other markets. Thus, for instance, trading in commodities presupposes the so-called money market as a source of standards for its transactions and operates within its embrace.

Take an even clearer example: Treat the factory pattern discussed as a physical, territorial entity, and its architectural diagram becomes a picture of a complex of nested enclosures, a sort of honeycomb figure. It expresses "layered" secondary territoriality. In accord with the latter concept, it depicts defended yet contingently accessible spaces. In fact, it shows spaces inside of spaces: walls or fences, or only parking lots or nice lawns, around buildings, the internal walls of which partition off rooms or shops or bays or cubicles or whatever, within which sectors of the open space are frequently in turn reserved for particular occupants and their equipment and activities. Traffic must pass through gates, or doors, or aisles among workbenches, counters, or desks.

The system represented by this architectural plan of an enterprise not only seethes with communication, it also confines and therefore restricts communication. The role of a room, as everyone who lives in a household ought to know, goes beyond just providing some space. Teenagers in particular know that a room's greatest asset is a closable door, which functions like the gate of a castle (we still are talking of "castles"!). In the scheme of spatial subdivision described, doors create privileged sanctuaries for dialog among only selected participants. "Let's discuss this in private" demands discrete venues.

Once again, rites of passage come into play. A guard post at the entrance of the factory compound, an information booth in the lobby, a receptionist in the office, a private secretary keeping watch at the boss' door—all obstruct whoever intrudes. Confrontations at each successive barrier call for tactful niceties and testimonials of serious business. The passwords exacted are not so arcane, and the vigilance is palpably less bristling, but the procedures differ little from those upon entering an army base or nuclear installation, or a sacred Shi'ite shrine.

The strategic implications of this sequestration of selected spaces, often hierarchically graduated, and of the consequent privacy, and therefore primacy, of communication that they can confer are enormous. They implement and guarantee a fundamentally political differentiation and disparity among the members of a society, or in fact within almost any collaborating social group. Accordingly, more discussion of them will be required (see Chapter 11), but it must await an exposition of the variations that can obtain in spatial arrangements in general. Unless the connections that go along with protected precincts are recognized, the major significance of the latter may not emerge, for their advantages are eminently communicative ones.

The picture just drawn of subdivided secondary territories "has strings attached." Communication lines connect any enterprise or institutional seat with other agencies on various networks and ultimately with a far-flung public, else its solipsistic existence would be pointless, its work force would evaporate, its unsolicited efforts would be futile, and its products or proclamations would literally go nowhere and serve no one. Privileged and often exclusive access to appropriate connecting strands on communication networks matters fully as much to an enterprise, or to virtually any institution, as does the reclusion of business in insulated venues.

Interactive relationships among discrete components drive change in the universe. Communication, as one class of them, as a whole must manifestly serve a function in the long run of evolution, that is, must have its repercussions on the world external to the individual, and in a way that yields some benefit. In other words, it has pragmatic functions. Communication organizes, instigates, and manages collective enterprise. Such common, coordinated activity, drawing on and drawing together the differentiated skills and powers of varied individuals, notably expands the productive potential, and hence the survival chances, of a human collectivity. By itself, such a proposition is hardly more than banal, but it does serve to highlight once more the importance of communicative interactions, which afford the only possible means of instituting effective collaboration.

Numerous animal societies avail themselves of efficient communicative devices in order to coordinate their common activity on behalf of enhanced survival possibilities. As remarked above, by far the most intensive employment of interindividual communication within the animal kingdom as a whole serves either mating activity, rank-order transactions, or territorial defense routines. Yet some creatures do use it otherwise. The provident ant and industrious bee, whom folklore and fable advise us to emulate, organize their tasks and interactions with gestural and object displays, including some that embody chemical stimuli. Many such insect species achieve a notable modification and stabilization of environmental conditions and can maintain huge populations fairly securely. But their exploratory interaction systems differ considerably from the expression used by human beings in communication.

The apparent immutability of insect displays and also the rigid regularity of the responses they evoke stand in contrast to the vastly greater fluidity and openness of human communication. Evidently the enduring structures built by some insect species, such as beehives and tropical termite nests, can induce persistent modifications of immediate physical environment. Furthermore, they may channel and condition individual activity by physical means to some extent, so that they do indeed serve to perpetuate given behavior patterns. Hence they may serve a time-transcending function of a sort. In addition, such social species abate territorial rivalry and conflict within the given community, presumably again through their characteristic communicative behavior. In the typical case, however, strangers from another nest or an alien species will meet with resistance and commonly annihilation. Some insects achieve their own form of transcendence and control, in other words, although in doing so their routines are apparently fixed and unchanging, and their responses to challenges invariably fixed.

If insect societies can build so efficiently and install enduring guidelines to behavior in their constructions, thus transcending temporal limitations, and if they maintain a partial territorial openness, are they really so different from human societies? Some of the sections above have identified lifelong learning as a distinguishing trait of humanity. Perhaps nowhere more than in the incomplete parallel with the insect societies just described does this feature stand out more clearly. For whereas the communicative devices developed by the social termites, ants, and bees depend on innate fixed responses to standardized stimuli, delivered in foreordained contexts, the conduct of human communication is decidedly open and variable, ever changing and free. The communicative capacities of a social insect are rigidly set by genetic inheritance and developmental chemistry. It could scarcely concern itself with its Geltung. We take "ant-hood" as antithetical to individuality.

Human beings, like members of many other species, manifestly require communication as a means of integrating individual activities into concerted enterprises of the group. Human communication, then, comprises the ultimate productive system that controls all the rest. If it were not possible, however, to assimilate labor and trade into our conception of communicative activity, as was proposed in a preceding section, then of course the communicative activity that instigates and manages production would appear as simply incidental and derivative. It would itself constitute just another subsidiary and restricted, although essential, branch of productive activity. Its instrumental role in coordination under a social division of labor might exhaust its significance.

The phrase "Time is money" tells something more about labor; about working for somebody else, in particular. It again brings out its fundamentally communicative character. For it is the employee's time, not really his or her physical work, that is bought. Presence counts more than performance; observant workers soon notice that arriving repeatedly late on the job is a more grievous sin than somewhat inept use of tools.

Not merely time is involved in hired toil, but also place and, yet more important, a special communicative relationship. It follows from the interpretation of work as communicative display that the very essence of labor consists in the worker's integration for a stated period of time into the dialog that constitutes production. In a typical factory dialog, an ongoing reciprocal blending of the management's verbal and the bench-worker's gestural performances produces material goods, for example.

The dialog employed is, of course, both directive and directional. The distribution of initiative is hierarchical, such that a flow of managed and differentiated activity proceeds downward, and another control flow moves upward, reporting on the operation. Each individual working in the system responds to particular cues or displays in order to fulfill his or her part. And the essence of the system consists simply and solely in each being on station and ready to participate according to the program of the enterprise. Communication takes care of the rest.

One often watches meticulous fingernail-filing and lip-painting operations in offices during slack periods. Those are okay: the word-processor operators sit ready to follow instructions that happen not to have come. Or once the shelves are stocked the clerks may plunge into a lengthy, searching critique of some basketball game on company time; quite all right again, as long as the boss doesn't need them.

It will surely not escape notice that the arrangements just described, if not the idle diversions, downright reek of rituality. The allocation of different speech patterns in the factory, office, or shop to different posts in the productive-communicative chain gives one nice indication. Striking, too, is the differentiation of dress between the coat-and-tie-strangled managers or flashily clad, overpainted secretaries in the front office and the longhaired, greasy-grimy guys down on the shop floor: they couldn't dream of changing places, dressed as they are. Yet more telling, the proportion of speaking to bodily action within a person's working performance often corresponds to relative rank and hints at the level of income. Less hard work and more words often equals more money.

Thus, the marks of distinction just noted not merely convey to an informed and sensitive observer an understanding of the functional differentiation of positions within the enterprise, but also provide a good incidental awareness of comparative status and its proportionate rewards. Not all meekly respectable clerks are well paid, of course, and not all scruffy roughnecks in the oilfields live on a pittance, but a crude correlation obtains between the ostentation going with a position and the income gained from it. In this regard, however, it should be noted that the comparative inviolability of the standards for dress, for example, within one sector of production, such as the factory floor, overrides the criteria applied by the general society and so may obscure the correlation between external appearance and relative affluence. This, though, is a matter of distinct diffusion domains and is enormously subtle.

Clearly, too, these patterns of enterprise relate to the secondary territoriality discussed in the previous chapter. An office or factory or shop is also, in its way, one of those "castles" that claim a distinct spatial and social jurisdiction and serve as centers of distinctive kinds of specialized activity. Admittance to them is selective. Each likewise is likely to participate in one or more connected spatial networks and perhaps hierarchies. And the population it serves will constitute another one of those rather indeterminate spatial constellations also previously discussed.

The discussion above has made much of spatial position within particular systems. The following chapter will now attempt to draw some more specific conclusions about its connection with Geltung and what we call, vaguely, personal power.

ELEVEN

Sources of Power •

Imagine your world as a chessboard. The field of the action is measured and marked. The persons, the pieces aligned in their places, are ranked in their powers. Moves are controlled by both rank and location. Dyadic encounters, each a minor rite of passage, determine their outcomes. The challenge of the game consists in employing the coordinated actions of the player's several varied resources in order to advance against obstacles, eliminate opposing forces, and finally neutralize the rival side and seize the Geltung of winning.

Success in a game of chess requires astute anticipation of any moves an opponent might make in response to each play. It calls for instant insight into all the spatial implications of every state of the board. A conclusively dominant position of checkmate confirms it.

The subtlety of chess reflects the differentiation of the spatial options allotted to the various pieces. Every piece possesses a distinctive Geltung of its own. Each can move, but only according to its rank, its allotted prerogatives. The king and the commoner-pawns alike are restricted, with one exception, to entry into squares adjacent to their own, but His Majesty, at least, unlike the poor pawns who can only march forward, can sidestep or judiciously retreat. The person of a king is sacrosanct; whoever might freely capture and touch it dethrones it and wins.

The queen's moves are freer than those of her mate. She can swoop in any direction over the board and wipe out whoever stands in her way. The castles or rooks, like ponderous engines of war, lunge directly ahead, or backward, or sideways, whereas neither of the two tricky bishops is nearly so straightforward, always sidling its eccentric way aslant back and forth. Most agile of all, the highly devious knights can leap over plodding sluggards, twist to the side, and pounce unexpectedly from cover.

The greatest lesson of this ancient game, however, teaches that all this versatility and power avails but little except when advantageous positions unleash it. The opponent always commands an array of identical pieces, so that Where and When, so to speak, matter more than do What or Who.

Chess is neither quite nature nor quite society, yet its microcosmic contention reflects the conditions that govern success and survival in both. For any creature, but especially for human beings, imbued as they are with expansive communicative propensities producing differentiating spatial consequences, relative position strongly predisposes an action to given results. Any halfwit can taunt a safely caged tiger.

In chess, any piece has its Geltung, exclusive alone to itself. Whatever its rank, any piece can capture a queen or checkmate a king. Everything hinges on the position it seizes, relative to other pieces. And so it is with humanity. Geltung redounds to position in venues: and Geltung is relative always. The spatial side of the game, be it chess or communication, thus is crucial. Space makes Geltung effective; Geltung not only generates spatial arrangements but also tries to exploit them. Any competent Master at chess ought to instantly see the point of this book.

Hierarchy hovers over the chessboard and heavily counts in the game. It does so likewise in life.

Franz Kafka's nightmare visions included some heartless hierarchies, in which the hapless supplicant was directed from one obscure office to another even more shadowy, vainly seeking a definite explanation of a terrifying cryptic accusation. Hierarchies often do impress those directed to them in a similar frustrating way, although but few could rival Kafka's *Castle*. That tormented writer's vague name for the institution that thus tortured his hero happens to have been the same as this account uses for institutional premises, which do indeed group into sometimes quite forbidding hierarchies.

Secondary territoriality pertains explicitly to the constructed facilities serving as an institution's seat. But territorial perimeter defense usually does not extend beyond the central site to enclose the whole surroundings. Instead, the institutional activities serve the population of a concentric and contiguous domain, innervated by its network of communications but devoid of formidable external boundaries. Such a zone might correspond to the extensive, imprecise foraging ranges of animals.

Although virtually anyone may pass unheeded, unhindered, and unharmed across their bounds, these service ranges do reflect a functional partitioning of space, to which there corresponds a multilevel structure of relationships among respective seats and service areas: a hierarchy. The Roman Catholic Church, for example, prototypically hierarchical, groups its parishes under bishoprics, and the latter under more inclusive national units, all subject finally to Rome; monastic orders of the church possess their own parallel hierarchical structure. Like arrangements recur in armies, business organizations, sporting associations, and widely elsewhere. Although certainly susceptible to geometric representation, however, and hence somehow spatial, a hierarchy itself hardly qualifies as a territorial order per se.

Not true territoriality, then, but a different spatial attribute of great importance, distinguishes the domains of hierarchical institutions: to wit, possession of privileged proprietary networks of communications, which do indeed partake of territorial exclusivity. A fair organic analogy would be a reticulated nervous system, with the seats of institutions its ganglia, threaded through cellular tissue, the mosaic of individual places. Just as in a living body, though, the separate circulatory systems of the blood and lymph and the alimentary pathways constitute distinct coexisting networks, so do the reticulations of varied institutions pervade a common geographic space.

A particular institution, however, may or may not construct and maintain a physical communication network of its own. The real interconnections in fact consist of actions and other natural processes rather than subsistent objects as such; an abandoned railway track connects precisely nothing to absolutely nowhere, and a telephone unused creates no contacts. Sporadic, not continual, the constitutive information flow follows whatever conduits best present themselves, be they the proprietary ones of a given institution or those open to use by everyone.

It accords with reality to regard not merely the communicative system as activity in space and time instead of a physical presence, but also to envision in like manner the hierarchy it sustains, and at last the very institution itself, despite its installation into a concrete, visible home. Activity is everything!

Nevertheless, hierarchical business avails itself of channels of communication such that it can when desired proceed in secrecy. Something similar to territorial exclusivity guards the traffic over those channels, whether its protective effect depends on outright physical insulation, cryptographic concealment, or yet other strategies. Together with selective restriction of access to institutional precincts themselves, the security of information channels completes the conditions for establishing a pervasive secondary territoriality.

Once long ago a cartoon appeared in a bold Polish magazine, showing two people standing at the edge of a grand public square. They were watching workers dismantle a heroic horseback statue of some erstwhile Great Leader. "Wait a minute, you!" cried one of the spectators. "Save the pedestal—we'll be needing it again!"

Power voids seldom last long. Someone is always around, ready to mount the political pedestal. We call that "coming to power." Just what does it stand for? Indeed, what is power?

Countless writers have tried to characterize power, far too many even to cite here (and we shall certainly disregard electric current, "brainpower," "firepower," "mechanical power," and all such irrelevant things). In lieu of borrowing a definition from anyone, let us test a conception of power, in accord with the terms of this book, as a particular kind of communicative relationship related in part to spatial position. This promises a highly informative new perspective.

Given the premise that any communication has a political side, evidently power is political too, whether explicitly so on a professional level or exerted in other domains of activity. The craving for Geltung, for recognition, respect, and influence, drives people to seek what we call power; and Geltung acquired can deliver it. Those who care enough for their Geltung dare to aspire; those who aspire seek to acquire it and exercise power.

Just what invests a communicative relationship with power? In a word, initiative, rooted in Geltung. The control of behavior that it signifies rests on priority in managing dialog, from giving the starting signal to having the last word, from setting agendas to getting reports. The capability of effectuating change in the world and society, by touching off chains of successive response in diffusion, demonstrates power. In exercising power an individual instigates actions by ultimate executors perhaps far removed from the source of the original initiative. This suggests a convenient means of measuring relative power: its magnitude would correspond to how many people someone can mobilize, or else perhaps to the degree of material change it ordains, or possibly again to the scope of its spatial manifestation.

The reader may already have surmised that, ironically, the more power a person possesses, in the political sense of the word employed here, the less personal muscle power and even brainpower that person will likely need to contribute to accomplishing a given task, and the greater the input of effort from other people will be. Approximately, as remarked somewhere above, an inverse proportion tends to obtain between power and exertion, or directing and sweating. That perhaps is why a vicarious gratification makes even mere "sidewalk superintendents" feel good.

When machines and automatic control devices get involved, the picture becomes yet more elaborate but the principle remains the same: almost unimaginable quantities of electrical, chemical, or mechanical energy often lie at the ready disposal of an operative who merely flicks a switch with a finger. To be sure, that kind of initiative does not belong solely to the average worker, for the operation hinges on directives (communicative initiatives, again) issued higher up in the system, where real power lies. In this manner, integrated into single systems of control, with initiative apportioned on a graduated basis and procedures sequentially organized, human enterprise can take charge of mighty natural forces.

A good deal more than simply a forceful personality has to undergird personal power, the privileged exercise of initiative to instigate or forward diffusion of commands and final execution of them. An impulse, for example, a directive, must follow established pathways of diffusion in a systematized fashion, as described in the previous chapter, in order to manifest power. This need not imply, of course, that personality makes no difference at all, as previous chapters examining this possibility will in fact emphatically show.

But recall that Napoleon could do no more than sit and brood and get sick once exiled to St. Helena. In contrast, during his earlier banishment to Elba he still had connections and so could conspire to return to remobilize France. His case well illustrates the need not merely for strength of personality but also for spatial advantage in order to get and hold power. The political capacity of eliciting compliance with an initiative does not float free in a void, it is anchored in space, and an individual's native political aptitude itself undoubtedly encompasses a strategic sense of spatial position that does not come into play only on battlefields. As a general, Napoleon had a genius for being in the right place at the right time, but the same could be said, too, of his political career generally: he repeatedly showed that he knew just when to rush to Paris and when to stay away.

As a feature of communication, then, power thus has to do with spatial relationships and involves the exercise of influence and initiative in a manner herein called political. Those generalities invite some examples.

Smoke-filled rooms, supposedly, were once where big political decisions got made. What happens now, with smoking in such great disfavor?

Get rid of the smoke though you may, most politicking, planning, bargaining, and major decisions still continue to occur within discrete, defended rooms and equivalent spaces. Just recall from a previous chapter the discussion of privileged precincts, constructed or construed to seal off those processes from general scrutiny or public participation. They tend to monopolize controlling initiative in many branches of human affairs, operating both as sequestered nests for political processes and as either primary centers of origin or "booster stations" for diffusing communication. In each case, their situation confers special power.

The same characterization would apply to rather larger spatial isolates that geographers, archaeologists, and anthropologists call cultural hearths. The latter simply consist of certain regions of the world in which new techniques have been perfected. Out of such centers of inventiveness, supposedly, have issued successive waves of influential impulses that, through imitative learning, spread cultural traits and whole complexes of traits far and wide.

Such would be, for example, the putative sites at which certain crop plants were first domesticated, or someone invented and retailed particular tools, songs, or myths—Central Mexico, probably, for maize, or New Orleans for jazz. Though not always requiring actual rooms to operate in, cultural hearths as well are somehow remote or sequestered enough to work things out on their own before they can diffuse them. Needless to say, no center could exist completely autonomous, however, and a good deal of back-and-forth exchange among creative centers of the sort may go on before the final product is arrived at; the story is likely not to prove altogether simple. The traditional manner of study of cultural diffusion has developed as a kind of detective game that seeks to solve such mysteries of origins.

The familiar spatial elements alluded to here collectively as rooms, or more broadly enclosures, infrequently stand entirely alone; they tend to be linked into systems extended in space, as detailed below. Their peculiar exclusivity, though, demands some prior consideration before discussion of systemic linkages.

The sequestered spaces of power appear concretely as defended, and most frequently constructed, venues devised to enclose and protect deliberations and diffusion initiatives. Obviously, though, the places concerned do not themselves exercise any power. According to the present reasoning, power must attach to interpersonal influence alone. Therefore it becomes apparent that the power conferred by enclosure, and with it connection, accrues alone to the living occupants of those sites. And the Geltung of the site and its occupant institution does, as it were, spill over onto the people it houses.

Furthermore, it manifests itself only at specific times. An abandoned castle ordinarily dominates no one, and an office shut for the night, even with all its array of tinkling telephones and ticking machines, merely serves if at all as a part of already established and programmed connecting communication. For action the people must be there.

And just who are these people? They can be anyone admissible, through appropriate rites of passage and reminders (tokens) thereof, to participation in the relevant activity. Their particular personalities may prove highly influential, and their specialist qualifications play a due part, yet neither of those two factors necessarily determines the personnel engaged in the proceedings within. The exercise of power falls to whoever gets invited or is allowed within. Influential action occurs in what we call the "exercise of office"—suggesting privileged location as much as the status. Power literally belongs to insiders.

Terribly ordinary and not always very well qualified or worthy people may insinuate themselves into the privileged company. At this time in history, with such recent strange goings on in the White House and Kremlin, and such deplorable conduct in corporate boardrooms and in vestries and mission schools, the foibles and worse of insiders are patent. Plainly the Geltung of places where power resides counts for more than the fallible personal qualities of their momentary incumbents. Spatial circumstances can often, as in the foregoing case, reveal something of why countries and societies get into trouble. It takes no cynic to see that power has not very much to do with virtue or wisdom or decency.

Yet some highly placed persons do show wisdom and decency. While president of the United States, Harry S. Truman reportedly kept a sign in view that read, "The buck stops here." At his desk in the Oval Office of the White House in Washington, he sat where the chain of blame ended. At the same time, of course, he also sat where the chain of command started.

A chain of command consists of a fixed system of authoritative directional circuits carrying orders downward from some supreme center via seried, insulated, privileged nodes. Again, the chain consists in fact of people ("officers" in business and the military) exercising subordinate but exclusive initiative according to rank.

The model corresponds rather closely to that of the central place hierarchy familiar to geographers, but one totally predominant branching command tree (notice the dendritic model turned on its head!) reaches down through the numerous nodes and their nested secondary territorial sectors. Thus, during war the headquarters of the Supreme Commander enjoy jurisdiction over the entire theater of operations, and each component army group, army, corps, division, brigade, regiment, battalion, and company within the force nests into its own respective spatial sector around its designated center, although all may be constantly on the move in the field. A particular officer alone performs the command or "line" (N.B.!) functions at each level, rather as workers on straight production lines do. Other officers carry out in aid of the former what are called "staff" functions and hence work outside the chain of command itself. Authority or power flows only through the single ramifying command channel.

A chain is only as strong as its weakest link, though, as people say, so that the personal qualities and qualifications of command personnel in a business or military system, as compared to other organizations, have an especially crucial bearing on operations.

Certain churches exhibit somewhat similar organizational patterns, and of course their vulnerabilities in regard to personnel are analogous. Likewise, state administrations tend to adopt similar spatial arrangements, although federalism, as against complete centralization, reserves considerable degrees of autonomy to subsidiary units.

The upside-down pyramid skeleton figure representing this form of organization instructs about relative power, among other things. Understandably, the higher up toward the apex a command position sits, the greater the power normally entrusted to its incumbent, and the wider the front or broader the field assigned to the unit. Would it be accurate to say, however, that this generalization also applies to the quality of personnel? Should the distribution of merit, character, and competence ideally conform to the pyramid's pattern?

Perhaps the answer to those questions could come as a surprise and reveal something important about organization in general. The public often adulates famous generals as "brave soldiers," when in fact they may not have been under fire for years. It simultaneously waxes sentimental over noble frontline fighters deeply dedicated to democracy, when in truth the soldiers' only urgent concern may be to keep from getting killed, protect their buddies as they can, and get the hell out of the area.

What soldiers have to do depends on where they find themselves within the combat zone (or behind it). Duties differ according to place, demanding differing talents and virtues. What makes a good supply officer in an army general hospital may not prove the stuff of battlefield glory, and most "grunts" in the infantry might make poor prospects for chaplaincies. The point of all this, of course, is that any human enterprise will call for diversified contributions, and that a successful orchestration of them must mobilize varying and even contrasting human qualities in people, then put them in the right places.

The personalities and skills appropriate for command in the military and management posts in business ("command presence," "executive talent," and so on) go along with only certain given enterprises and their power allocations. In a university, for example, in contrast to an army or a bank, the opportunity to discover and debate (and publish) counts more, at least among the faculty, than does managerial skill. Although the general North American public appears to revere the deans and directors more than they do the most creative cranks on the campuses, the latter impress their peers most and will presumably also retain their reputations longer. Unlike the ephemeral mandates of a mere administrator, the diffusional power of an able researcher or teacher can continue to instruct and inspire for generations.

Nevertheless, the scale of rewards to achievement and effort in a university appears to conform to the pyramid's shape. The trouble is not simply that the very administrators are the ones who administer salaries. This common arrangement rests on a much more plausible communications rationale, unfortunately for professors. Compensation tends to correspond to hierarchical level within a command structure, and hence to the number of people for whom responsibility goes with the position. A harried yet still compassionate and clever dean may really deserve more money than a profound and pampered but petulant philosopher.

Try this little exercise. Make a ramifying line graph of the network of an institution, showing the flows of information from, through, and to each node. Determine by inspection the volume of information traffic that each particular node either originates or has charge of. If you then assign a numerical rank to each node according to the volume shown, it should closely correspond to the magnitude of the respective remuneration and perquisites of each office.

Another indicator would be the sum of terminal nodes a given display initiator reaches in a fixed period. Pay and privileges tend to increase nearly in direct proportion to the number of people depending on an individual's initiative. That initiative may in fact mostly consist of the retransmission of routine displays, but it suffices, nevertheless, to scale the rewards.

How extensive an area, how large a spatial domain, does an individual's authority take in? The answer most likely will tell you as well the level of income enjoyed by each recipient, compared with co-workers.

And how hard does an individual labor? Look at an index to that and you find that exertion and expense of care do not harvest richly. Muscle is cheap and mouths are expensive. As preceding chapters have said, the ordinary workers in factory, field, office, or retail shop sell obedience more than power, time more than talent, energy more than inspiration. Nowhere for long has the cheapness of their toil changed very much as against that of those who direct them. The nefarious relations of production denounced by Marx did not reverse in the Soviet Union.

Highly skilled labor commands a return in proportion not only to what technique contributes in itself to the product, but also to how many fellow workers follow directions from the technicians and have to await their signals—on the line, perhaps—to get on with their tasks. Thus a strictly technical hierarchy exists alongside the managerial one and interlaces with it, and it also reaps the corresponding returns, according to level of technical authority.

What about the experts and professionals whose labor, done skillfully, deals with material things, not just words? What measures their contributions and how are they paid for them? Certainly not sweat alone nor simply hours spent at work procure them their preference. Their virtual irreplaceability furnishes one basis for their special claims to income. Even so, by and large, many of them still deliver their product in words or similar displays, such as architectural drawings, engineering reports, legal opinions and cases, or scientific lectures or publications, and these alone entitle them to reward.

Such specialists ordinarily must emerge from stringent rites of passage in order to practice their callings. The very certification that this affords entitles them to special compensation. And the process of qualifying does certainly involve intense, prolonged labor.

Professional and expert work, in addition, earns returns on authority. A librarian, physician, engineer, or scientist directs others, although often privately. Such qualified, certified specialists radiate advice and commands to a respectful clientele, largely through channels on institutional networks at hand, or directly through face-to-face interaction with numerous people who form a kind of constellation around them, not dissimilar to that attained by broadcasts. The scope of that constellation and its durability aid in determining recompense.

Geltung gets a person inside those privileged centers of power, the "smoke-filled rooms" that control so much of societies' doings, and into physicians' clinical redoubts as well. It both opens and closes protective doors on the beneficiary's behalf.

Geltung attributed to place, introducing an individual into the wider networks of diffusion, may vastly magnify the consequences of whatever displays that person may utter. Communicative power bestows political power, not just in party and government spheres. It enables its possessor to manage everyday enterprise conducted conjointly by numbers of people. Again, in this instance, substantial Geltung both adheres to superordinate positions in a hierarchy and conversely stands as a requisite for promotion into them. Public political positions exhibit analogous features. As always, though, Geltung derives from appearances, no more, and need not certify worthiness or competence.

Not long since, a certain very military colonel reputed for derring-do arrived in the underground chambers of power and wielded an influence out of proportion to rank, abetted by access to inner councils and secret channels of command. When a showdown came in the Congress, however, a show of personal integrity became the issue rather than the Geltung of his somewhat illicit subterranean position or the ambiguous fame of his allegedly conspiratorial deeds, and "this colonel" came off pretty well. The Geltung accruing from position, association, or exploits, prominent or privy to few, can sometimes evaporate suddenly and leave its rueful ex-owner to purvey alternative displays. Thus Geltung lives in eternal peril of abrupt cancellation: *sic transit gloria mundi*, and likewise *sal si puedes*: get out if you can.

In blessed, bountiful British Columbia we have a habit of referring to our legislative politicians by the term, "The Honourable" So-and-So. (Disregard the Anglophilic spelling, please, but notice the quotes: it is not "the honourable *so-and-so*," despite the numerous improprieties in office revealed by some recent resignations and cases in court.) This usage extends to publicity, including the billboards announcing new government construction projects under the name of the minister in charge. Well, on the very day after a recent election, the minions of the victorious opposition went around and removed the names of the former ministers, but left "The Honourable" still in place, waiting.

Like the Polish cartoon and the pay scales of deans that I mentioned somewhere above, this instance illustrates the Geltung that sticks tenaciously to standing in hierarchical systems. It has reasons to, as also admitted. Nowhere does this principle express itself more tellingly than in the structures of great institutions. Now let the next chapter examine some samples, to wit the churches and sovereign states.

TWELVE

Limits of Force •

The British Empire once, as Kipling put it, held "dominion over palm and pine." A nice bit of imperialistic botany! Yet dominions tend to diminish distressingly quickly, and the Empire has shrunk to a handful of scattered islands. Nevertheless, somebody still holds dominion over each of the lands that Britain once proudly ruled, and some of their inhabitants might accuse even those present masters of imperialism. Sovereign states, now nearly two hundred in number, continue to split up the world among themselves and leave nothing over but brine in the oceans. In fact they even encroach on the seas, for some distance out, more and more.

Map those sovereign spatial divisions and you make a statement of political relationships and, above all, communicative ones. Most other spatial structures and forms will prove subsidiary to those voluminous patterns. They will tend to envelop most institutions. And each country's borders will define a world unto itself, leaving humanity fragmented.

What kind of territoriality is this? The division of the globe among states does not represent the same primary territoriality found in the case of the family home, for it serves entirely dissimilar functions. It also amounts to something a good deal more imperious than the vague secondary spatial claims of most institutions, imposing itself firmly on everyone who falls within its compass. It amounts to a tertiary territoriality. With it, uniquely, goes government, a prevalent system of power relationships backed up by force.

The previous chapter advocated the principle that power consists of communicative advantage, that is, of control of initiative. Prudently used, that advantage itself permits the further accrual of Geltung to the individuals and institutions that possess it. If that be the case, it is the power of communication—bearing the Geltung of reason, justice, and mercy as much as that merely of physical dominance—that constructs the state and conducts any government's operations. Yet the very force that always broods behind assertions of sovereignty communicates a message only too well. The sovereign power of states, in fact, resides at the final extreme in intimidation, after all purely a matter of communication. The looming threat of force confers its own sinister Geltung, despite the impracticality of outright annihilation of all opposition. No regime, however bloodthirsty, can survive by doing away with all of its people!

Niccolò Machiavelli understood profoundly the real underpinnings of government power. It was he who counseled systematic terror as an indispensable means of securing control of a state. He explained how to cow a population into compliance with government dictates. Throughout history, nevertheless, and notably during the dissolution of the dictatorial regimes of Eastern Europe, the Soviet Union, and Latin America in recent years, personal bravery and defiance of government threats have repeatedly overturned oppressive overlords. All the force commanded by any regime, tyrannical or not, is finally impotent before determined refusals to capitulate to it, once they succeed in galvanizing great masses of people.

Recall that every human dialog depends on freedom of response for its realization. That inherent freedom is dramatized when people cease enough to dread danger and dare to answer the challenge of force with personal sacrifice. As a result mighty states eventually crumble. Patrick Henry's cry of "Give me liberty or give me death!" and the *gritos*, or outcries, of leaders of Mexico's struggle for independence, diffusing, emboldened the people to revolt and sweep away their oppressors.

All sovereign systems must rely on force, or rather the threat of it, to support their authority. But although some writers attribute a so-called monopoly of force to the state, probably no such a thing has ever been achieved completely. One reason lies in the physical impossibility of police or the military being everywhere at once. Dissidence can thrive almost in their shadow and break out in the open whenever their backs are turned.

In view of this limitation, official agencies often promote the diffusion of respect and fear of their force by staging strategic displays of repression and punishment, reports of which, circulating through a population, may help to stultify organized resistance and stifle public protest. Open protest and direct assault on the state may abate in consequence, but no country can free itself by such means, or probably any other, from ordinary crime and brigandage, which may themselves have historically provided one congenial seedbed for revolt. Furthermore, citizen outrage at excesses perpetrated by a state can itself diffuse widely and work at last to undermine the system. Perhaps, however, plain dissatisfaction with declining conditions of life and livelihood, widely communicated, will ordinarily light the final spark that ignites an explosion.

A second source of vulnerability inheres in the very agencies of force. Who will police the police? Not all is always concord and cooperation among the armed agencies of violence. Military coups as often as not overturn ruling military officers. Intrigue and rivalry tend to afflict almost any organization and when provided with weapons can themselves impel rebellion and takeovers, or sometimes simply anarchy. Of this fact, Afghanistan and the former Yugoslavia provide the grisliest examples at this moment in 1995. The effects of all the foregoing factors in concert have, as even current history illustrates, frequently culminated in the downfall of supposedly secure entrenched regimes. What ever became of the *nerushimyĭ soiuz*, or unbreakable union, glorified in the former Soviet national anthem?

The state is a state of mind. As a creature of communication, the sovereign state is no substance, but merely a rather uneasy state of affairs or condition of dialog. In this respect, its nature is identical to that of all institutions, consisting of countless ongoing dyadic interactions among individuals. Constantly enacted in pageantry as well as routine proceedings, it only exists as long as its agents can perform convincingly in such a manner that it holds and uses initiative in dialog. Total inaction is lethal to it, any assertion of authority is better than none.

States, notwithstanding, truly represent power: sovereign, pervasive, deadly persuasive real power. They dominate the crucial communications responsible for public order, and through them govern the ordinary conduct of affairs. Through diffusion, their administrations regulate (or shelter from regulation!) the uses of the land, resources, and technical equipment and, to quote the American Constitution, in some fashion everywhere purport to "form a more perfect Union, establish justice, insure domestic tranquility, provide for the common defense, promote the general welfare, and [only sometimes] secure the blessings of liberty" for the population. The very prescriptions that then follow in that exemplary constitution indicate the method elected for achieving those ends: dialog, disciplined within the carefully balanced institutional framework ordained, a formal political order.

While specifying a certain political process, the United States Constitution likewise gives recognition to space, for it enumerates respective initiative powers allotted to the federal level, the states, and the people at large; the Bill of Rights goes further still in circumscribing interference with individual expression and autonomy. Most if not all constitutions or their juridical counterparts define spatial jurisdictions, institute political dialog, and allocate prerogatives in some analogous way.

The supremacy of such political-administrative institutions, with the lesser counterparts that nest hierarchically under them, universally obtains within the established spatial jurisdictions that divide the dry land surface of the earth and seas adjacent. But such states do not quite equate to nations. No guaranteed spatial jurisdiction attaches to a nation as such, and it need not even govern itself. A nation can survive dispersed or divided spatially, or deprived of freely functioning institutions, or dominated almost totally by strangers. Thus it need not cease to constitute a cultural entity and likewise a communicative one. It will not necessarily boast its own state and may or may not claim a country of its own. The Romany (Gypsies) and, until recently, the Jews had stood as classic cases of dispersed nations domiciled among others and dominated by them; they kept alive largely by assiduously maintaining their own autonomous communication networks.

Also, more or less oblivious to state regimes, many small, remote, and isolated populations throughout the world go on governing themselves without much benefit of outside intervention, although clearly decreasingly so. They constitute not only distinctive cultural regions but separate, if nominally subordinate, political realms as well. Within the often miniscule jurisdictions they succeed in asserting, such out-of-the-way indigenous "countries" possess their own communicative connections, sometimes hierarchical, and institutional centers and diffusion fields. Anthropologists tend to deny them the distinction of counting as states, but nonetheless numerous small bands and tribes around the world do carry on political and administrative functions comparable to those of more elaborate polities.

To have a country is not equivalent to merely inhabiting a country. Every "country" nowadays in practice implies a state, with every human individual a subject or a citizen of one. In theory, even unadministered aborigenes fall under their sway. These countries constitute a now closed set of territories of a special kind, spatial entities that often overlie and override the boundaries of cultural domains, linguistic and religious realms, and topographical divisons, much to their ultimate peril. The present international order rests on and supports their primacy, despite the forces that increasingly contest it.

The restless forces of religion and ethnicity that work against the unity imposed by many states are worthy of examination in their own right, which would however exceed the scope of this book. Here, I can only strongly urge the reader to consult a most imaginative, informative, and comprehensive, and likewise highly unorthodox, discussion of the rise, composition, and fall of ethnic entities as a function of human energy, published first, of all places, in the Soviet Union (Gumilev, 1990).

The communication system of a state can dictate much of the character of its landscapes, for the dispositions of the system govern the placement and potency of various networks, the allotment of spatial domains to numerous institutions, and thus the flux of cultural influence and the enterprise of transformation of environments. Along international and even provincial boundaries, road surfaces and building styles and even crops frequently sharply contrast. A significant relationship obtains between communication and the landscape that this indicates.

As they approach such a major boundary, people's observable behavior often manifests a certain deference and ceremoniality, for crossing entails a considerable rite of passage. Understandably so, for at many an international boundary individuals undergo something almost analogous to baptism, an ordinarily perfunctory ritual that inducts them into legitimate and legal participation in the life of another state. Thereby they acknowledge themselves as subject to the law of the land in that country.

If "the law is an ass," it is also an asset, assuring that everyone included within a given society accepts at least a basic few common rules of behavior and judgment, like it or not.

Politics in the professional sense stops, purportedly, where law begins. Indeed, any so-called political contamination of legal activity provides grounds for weighty reproof, despite the reality that the political process never stops anywhere that people interact. One can easily observe the distinction between formal, highly routinized and repetitive legal proceedings and the often improvised and highly informal processes of politics infusing ordinary communication, but the former always include the latter. It ought to be noted, apropos, that legislative business, especially, comprises a fascinating blend of political with legal forms of activity.

What happens in courtrooms depends on Geltung and dyadic displays just as much as what happens in bedrooms. Although the composition of the venues differs dramatically (to say the least!), encounters in court and in (modern day) courtship conform to identical dialog formats, featuring reciprocating provocations (indeed!) and frequent unexpected twists and turns, although each tends to reveal quite different things. In both those cases and in all human dialog, somewhat unpredictable optional interactions stemming from the mutual process of stimulation by two living people, each full of idiosyncracies, shape and deliver the outcome.

Systems of law are the hard bones of the state: judges, lawyers, and police perhaps its muscles. A corpus of laws today consists of accretions from various sources—legislation, previous judgments, traditional customs—compiled into codes and records of cases. A rather ossified stucture, it serves as a skeleton does to provide some kind of spare but rigid frame on which the social fabric may be hung.

However, Hammurabi came late. Laws or their equivalents existed long before tablets for writing them down on, and effective systems of law prevail today among illiterate peoples beyond the reach of state courts. Tribal elders and traditional chiefs in places on nearly every continent continue to administer justice in their fashion. Religious law, so important in the European Middle Ages, likewise continues in full application in many countries, such as certain Islamic ones. Many great institutions, moreover, both legislate and enforce their own rules, wherever not preempted by the public laws. Predictable systematic guides to interpersonal behavior are everywhere indispensable.

The law is compulsory culture. The bulk of the residue called "culture" that lodges in a region washed across by countless diffusions is a highly diversified, almost chaotic composite, affecting each individual a little differently. The law contrasts with other aspects of culture, however, in applying bindingly to everyone within the territorial jurisdiction in which it is valid, and also in its almost complete standardization. Furthermore, it has the Procrustean property of applying even in regions within the state in which it is not culturally endemic. No better example could exist than that of aboriginal people deemed subject to, say, Canadian law, whose observance of some of their own customs leads almost automatically to trouble with the law of their province, and disproportionate incarceration.

Even in the grateful absence of capital punishment, imprisonment imposes a harsh penalty. Whatever the stigma with which it diminishes the prisoner's Geltung, it deprives individuals of the spatial mobility identified in this book as an urgent, unceasing natural need of a human being. Involuntary confinement in addition curtails the options of communication, surely equally important. It furthermore divests the inmates of another precious thing, the freedom to make their own decisions, even regarding most intimate things. They are constantly told what to do and not asked for comment; they must answer with only obedience. In these three ways, living in captivity abridges or abolishes individual autonomy drastically and severely constricts the scope of possible communication.

Captives can always respond with open defiance of orders, of course, and sometimes they do. They still have that fundamental freedom native to dialog. But the system is subtle. Wardens and guards do not desire martyrs; they can simply totally isolate any refractory inmate. In less supposedly enlightened times, a prisoner's obdurate refusal to conform to directions, to convert to a loathed religion or confess to alleged conspiracy, for example, elicited gruesome retributions. In such situations, the captive might at least triumph through martyrdom. That honorable although fatal recourse to communicative freedom and dignity is mostly denied to prisoners today in Western lands, although certainly not everywhere. Color some parts of your world map in blood.

But all the subjects of a modern state also live, in a way, confined, even though under far less onerous conditions. A government outright imposes its laws and jurisdictions on a permanent and compulsory basis without awaiting the acquiescence of each inhabitant of its territories. Citizens by birth, at least, have no choice, unless they emigrate. Save when domestic eruption or foreign conquest intervenes, the supreme authority of the state is always simply assumed and duly enforced.

Nonetheless, any state system must eventually somehow come to terms with the pressures brought by its subjects. Sheer force may suffice for a while, but as described above, accumulating widespread dissension and disaffection will at last find expression. Harsh and rigid systems then crack and crash, whereas more humane and flexible ones can bend to accommodate the inevitable.

Legislative mechanisms offer one means of such conciliation and compromise that may preserve a state, if not its current policies. Another is the ballot box that summarizes people's preferences.

Voting constitutes yet another complex rite of passage, for citizen and candidate alike. Its communicative function purportedly finally guides the destinies of whole societies. Specific and subtle spatial arrangements manage it. And Geltung in this, as in so many matters, is paramount.

"History is bunk!" said Henry Ford. As a devotee and promoter of progress, he may have supposed that every day, in every way, things get better and better, so why should history matter? He may have been right; but now that painful misgivings begin to set in regarding such contemporary signs as the fractionation of state allegiances, the unsoundness of global and national economies, the decline of civic morality, and the rampages of unleashed technology, we almost flinch in the face of the future that we can foresee. And history holds precedents in plenty for today's cruel dismay.

Just situate yourself in third- or fourth-century Rome, as contention, corruption, nepotism, and extravagant ambition gnaw at the roots of its glory. Read Gibbon's dire tale! Mercenary barbarians infest the army, the rigor of schooling declines, the Latin language begins to decay, and imports from far provinces replace the produce of Italy's farms. Their Geltung having evaporated, the voices of authority are discredited; ancient, trusted institutions crumble. With leadership dispersed, riots and wars rage within. As conditions of orderly, reliable diffusion disappear, a long-lasting crisis ensues.

The rise of Christianity, diffusing in from the East, occurs just in time to salvage something of stability but cannot restore Rome's full felicity and creativity. Each region is remote from every other, in contrast to the well-knit Roman world. Things do indeed eventually settle down, but only into hermitages, monasteries, hamlets, and heavily fortified castles, mostly at odds one with another. Byzantines and Arabs nearly monopolize industry, commerce, science, and scholarship. Ecclesiastical organization and doctrine diffuse, to be sure, but in the West much of the Classical heritage hibernates until the Renaissance. Many centuries elapse before the vigor of the West then reasserts itself. Some people now see this familiar story as an object lesson.

The details of Rome's decline and fall would amply document the hazards of diffusion. Another good example is afforded in church history. Looking back to earlier councils, heresies, schisms, and apostasies, it is easy to detect the instability of ecclesiastical systems. The Christian community has repeatedly fragmented into regional sects and establishments as bishops rebelled and broke out of the fold to set up their own systems, or preachers deviated from the current doctrine and were expelled with their flocks. Secular powers often abetted division. From successive reformations, new revelations, and sectarian separations in general have descended the multifarious churches of today. Which line of descent is legitimate?

Wisdom and politeness both dictate that one should not speak too freely in company about religion and politics. I might instead have discussed other examples, such as leveraged buy-outs and overseas branch plants, or ethnic eruptions and separatisms. Any such case will illustrate that human institutions do not last forever, do not hold together, do not unyieldingly resist the powerful, sometimes divisive forces of individual Geltung and the strains of spatial extension.

Such declines and downfalls as history shows to mark the careers of religions and states may seem like the gravest problems humanity faces, but they surely are not. The Geltung of any human institution rises or falls at last according to its capability of dealing with far more important issues. The challenges amd dangers confronting the species worldwide today have assumed a magnitude such that they promise to tear states to shreds and smother religions in doubt or a desperation that will turn them into self-deluding lunatic cults.

Intelligence, insight, and their free expression may somehow prevail in spite of the institutional crisis, but only if lucky enough to seize on the factors responsible for some dreadful prospects that humanity faces. I can only with due humility suggest that possibly an understanding of how the species communicates, and what that behavior entails and results in, can help to illuminate choices still open. I therefore propose the Geltung Hypothesis as one clue to what has gone wrong, but preferring always to hope for a far-sounder analysis able to show things aright. Humanity, free, must somehow learn to be wise.

Neither state nor religion can help us enough; now all is up to the individual person, as really always was true.

The two concluding chapters briefly summarize some of the larger dimensions of the global social and environmental situation now looming and suggest the bearing on them of the argument presented in this book.

THIRTEEN

• Borrowed Energies

$\mathbf{A}$s far as we know, some day the sun will explode. Before that, the earth at some point is likely again to turn inhospitable to any living being. Until then, organic evolution will continue, and in time selection will certainly eliminate the human species. Long in advance, every nation now flourishing will dissolve and disappear, and every city crumble to dust. The pitiless apocalyptic riders will return again and again to lay peoples low. Today's institutions will rapidly shrivel and be replaced. Proud wealth and power will perish betimes. Our own mortality stalks us and will strike each one of us down all too soon.

What a dismal prospective! Its inescapable truth is no solace. Nothing will stay the cosmic events that are destined to swallow the solar system. No conceivable measures can halt evolution forever. Never could any people or society aspire to eternal existence. Everyone is mortal. It takes no pessimist to recognize that everything must pass away.

Those brooding certainties cannot, however, dissuade humanity from hope. Vitality, the force of life, bravely laughs in their face. Faith—in eternal salvation, serene release in Nirvana, humanity itself, or just in ourselves—reassures us and spurs us to confident action. Love and compassion and trust enlighten it.

Still more pressing immediate problems confront the world and the species, and attention to them must absorb humanity in urgent practical concerns. As if not content to contemplate the cosmic cataclysms in store, the species creates its own crises and hazards. With those it can deal. With those above all it must deal.

Some impudent voices from time to time have announced the imminent conquest of nature. Clarence Glacken (1967) has shown that such grandiose predictions recur intermittently in human history. Struggles and stratagems do occur, yes; but no conquest, if such be assumed, will ever endure.

The nature to which we belong is certainly not the enemy. For one thing, it includes our human bodies and selves; therefore, no matter how keenly people might long to free themselves from nature, to rise above it, they simply cannot. They can only exploit the natural potentialities within themselves in order to better their lot. In some modest fashion, insight and action, culture and social endeavor can delay the day of reckoning with unpropitious natural forces. Human intelligence, whose resourceful spy is science, can worm its way into the secrets of nature and sometimes predict its operations in time to plan adaptations. Enlightened efforts may be able to muster the disciplined strength of the species to collaborate in fighting to survive. Personal Geltung can serve as a tool to mobilize work toward earthly redemption.

The most promising tactics for self-defense of humanity assuredly consist of attack on immediate problems, combined with probes and regroupments to anticipate the next advantageous advance. The spatial disposition of forces must readily adjust to current situations and avoid rigidity.

The cyclical rhythms of nature proceed without special heed of the needs of humanity. We can only adapt. There will always be weather and storms, earthquakes, eruptions, droughts, floods, and fires that defy our control and scourge our communities. Human beings can do little more than take cover and help one another when smitten. Yet that mutual help can go far, and the systems of nature yield bounty when properly courted. Their spectacular energies they lend to humanity lavishly, once rightly addressed. But we only borrow the power that grows our crops, drives our engines, and sustains our comforts. Humanity survives on nature's loans.

Remember the parable (Matthew 25; Luke 19) of the master who lent to his servants and, returning, rewarded those who had used the loan wisely and rebuked the one who only had hoarded it? The most magnanimous of loans may remain unutilized or be squandered or ill employed. When humanity avails itself of nature's diverted powers, it sometimes does so recklessly and thriftlessly and faces an ultimate penalty.

Sun and rain benefit crops but, not used with care, erode and dessicate the land. Running water and wind remove the wastes of manufacture, traffic, and metabolism, yet when loaded beyond certain thresholds, instead they concentrate and redistribute them dangerously. As the energies that drive machines increase, greedy exploitation using them becomes able to despoil and exhaust resources. The more freely and widely human beings can roam with the help of natural fuels, and the greater the destructive power of either their workaday tools or their weapons becomes, the more their fellow species seem fated to decline and the worse the violence visited upon humanity itself.

Environmental disruption and violation of habitat systems occur not because of absolute, ubiquitous abuse of natural potentialities, but rather of misapplications specific to the given place and time. The relevant technological dimensions of human agency may either reveal themselves to study in advance or come vividly to light with ongoing experience. Technology, after all, entirely depends on consulting and accepting nature as it is. But incorrect or injudicious applications of technical knowledge and means, out of place or untimely or excessive in magnitude, turn it and nature against us. The personal Geltung of individuals and the derivative Geltung of institutions enable some of them to summon up social effort and technical means enough to possibly exceed the safe tolerances of habitats. The pursuit of Geltung itself can turn into the sort of vanity or greed that encourages those who hold such great power to disregard the ultimate consequences of their initiatives for the rest of humanity. Thus our human craving for Geltung can itself menace collective welfare or even survival. Humanity cannot blame nature outside of ourselves for its problems. But our agency in nature works to our advantage when properly managed, lending us access to spectacular energies.

Flick the switch and the lights go on, as currents surge along the electrical system all the way down from a dam in the mountains; twist a tap and out trickles water; bury a seed and it sprouts. These instances illustrate that in general human agency consists primarily of turning nature's forces on and off.

Nature consists just of such forces. To the senses, the universe seems to be solid and durable, but in fact only "change" can describe the reality we ordinarily experience. Its great cyles of energy-transfer account for its state and even apparent composition at any given moment, but each such condition is only transitory. Eternal fluxes of energy apparently constitute the only deeper reality within the space and time we commonly envision, although fundamental physics and cosmology have begun to reveal even grander concepts of a quantum universe where all might be otherwise.

Yet an account of natural fluxes of energy as manifested on the earth can already yield a consistent and thoroughly satisfying understanding of the natural order that human beings encounter and its relation to the lives of human beings, as a recent book by Vaclav Smil (1991) has impressively shown.

Nothing alien to humankind, nature dwells in our innermost selves, and likewise we dwell within nature. Humanity swims in its circulations and plunges a calculated yet infinitesimal controlling impulse decisively into their motions. The magnificent fluxes of light and thence heat from the sun; the movements of magma that even make continents migrate; restless electromagnetic fields; chemical reactions; the currents of oceans and atmosphere; the journeys of water through oceans and air and over and under the ground; the small transmigrations of substances building the soil; the mingling of water, minerals, and air in the life processes of living plants; the activities of animals at every level: all these and yet more interpenetrating cycles can, through human ingenuity, be trapped and trained and turned to use.

Technology borrows its forces from nature and returns them in due course. Human labor either alone or with the intermediary of tools, including machines, as well as certain facilities constructed within an environment, can divert, constrain, and direct the energies moving the natural cycles and use them in turn to move and modify material substances (Wagner, 1960). The first, most fundamental capture of energy takes place when individuals, like any animal, ingest and digest the food that nature provides them. The body soon disperses the calories acquired back into nature once more through physical activities and other bodily processes. A somewhat similar metabolic regime marks the borrowing of other kinds of energies than those stored in foods.

With adequate nourishment the human body, working alone, can contend with the basic tasks of survival if necessary, once instructed and equipped through other human beings' efforts, and with their cooperation. In fact, a bare majority of the world's people do still subsist more or less in this manner. Even the poorest and most isolated, though, have benefited for countless generations from their predecessors' experience and learned to shape the means and procedures they need for securing some sort of livelihood.

Let us forego a recital of all the technicalities of the numerous forms of productive activity conducted in even just one society. It would stretch the reader's patience beyond its fair limits. Plenty of descriptions of them exist, in any case. The real relevance of humankind's selective management of nature to the present discussion centers on its communicative aspects.

Patently, provisional control of natural energies would ordinarily presuppose concerted enterprise on the part of some group of people, if not in conducting the work involved, at least in determining means for doing it. You can certainly strike a fire for yourself, but who showed you how? Who gave you the matches or bow drill?

When individuals do act in concert they have moreover to establish appropriate spatial arrangements, such as some of those described in previous chapters, and allocate power in such a fashion that human initiative can effectively anticipate and dominate the behavior of the natural energy flux. Any very productive and prolonged exploitation of natural energies or just materials requires that the users systematize their operations and put them under orderly management. Hierarchical systems arise to diffuse instructions and coordinate activities. Traditional and newly invented methods pass down and around by diffusion to guide the solitary efforts of independent farmers or builders, cooks or workers in crafts.

Within the context of labor, remember, every action not only produces but also figures as a display. Furthermore, whenever the work of an isolated individual attracts the attention of peers, it too becomes subject to response in the manner of any display. The techniques learned and applied by a person in work or even a game fall subject, like any matter diffused, to scrutiny and commentary. Try to play through a solitaire game where other people are present and not have them kibitz!

Only by virtue of diffusion of invented methods and artifacts, diffusion of organizational directions, and even diffusion of kibitzers' comments does humanity acquire and maintain successful techniques of dealing with nature. The results appear in a comprehensive spatial reorganization. Human occupation changes the ecological balance and spatial arrangements, eliminating or marginalizing certain previous species, introducing new opportunities for other ones, creating entire new genetic lines, transforming the soil, altering the chemical character of air and water, and of course installing its own distinctive artificial components into the environment. The work of Alfred Crosby (1987) affords an impressive illustration of how the diffusion resulting from contact of people can alter environments—in his instance, the opening of the Americas and the Antipodes to the greater world.

The intervention of humanity often produces physical effects that quantitatively transcend the normal thresholds of natural processes and introduce qualitatively novel phenomena, such as the extensive pollution of air, land, and water all too familiar at present. That important side of the matter, becoming well documented by now, need not detain this discussion, which must concentrate on communication. In fact, for all the study devoted to environmental alteration and its frequently alarming consequences, the character of human agency itself remains the least understood, but also the most crucial element. This book responds to the conviction that only a more adequate appreciation and analysis of humanity's behavior in ecological terms—and that, as I hope is now clear, indicts communication and the consequent role of personal initiative—can make sense of our faltering stewardship of this earthly environment.

Environment can signify simply "the surroundings, wherever one is." That hasty definition would do as well for region, habitat, or landscape, depending on the emphasis sought. It therefore cannot stand as it is. Nowadays everyone among our contemporaries seems preoccupied about environment. Presumably their concerns have stemmed from alarm at degraded habitats or dismay at desecrated landscapes. Why then instead the talk of "environment"?

The answer relates to the major cycles of nature just mentioned. These scoff at mere regions, for they can make them and break them, and do not respect the limits that people assign. They toy with our habitats unrestrainably. They repaint and rearrange our landscapes as pitilessly as a harried insecure homemaker redoes the house. Atmosphere, hydrosphere, biosphere, and all the rest are global in extent and activity, disdainful of delimitation.

The seamless environment is one, indivisible. That which surrounds us and squeezes us hard has no bounds. It smothers the earth in one great tightly woven blanket. The ultimate system, it encompasses even the heavens in a single interactive entity. What happens anywhere within it can have its repercussions everywhere; when scientists sound their alarms about global warming or ozone depletion, they illustrate this principle. Erratic occurrence of rainfall in America and apparently even in Africa, in defiance of seasonal norms, reveals the influence of the distant El Niño current off Peru. The dust of Philippine volcanoes tints remote skies.

Bring commerce, custom, and technology into the picture, and their crucial bearing on environment becomes equally evident. The consequences of diffusive communication profoundly affect people anywhere. Humanity, remember, has always held at least loosely together in a single universe of diffusion, no matter how slowly it functioned. People since the beginning have migrated, interbred, and learned to imitate their neighbors. But their expansion, proliferation, and ever-increasing technical proficiency introduce risks. Thus, as misgivings about the effects of nuclear tests on the weather remind us, and a negative national balance of payments proclaims, environment has fateful economic, technological, and cultural aspects, too. Whatever we choose to regard as artificial or "social" belongs to the natural whole.

Any habitat reflects the net effects of distant environmental events, as just stated. In human perspective, their impact may register as either beneficial or disadvantageous. Although human inventiveness and the cooperative effort fostered by widespread communication can already to some extent mitigate local effects induced by human activity, global physical phenomena, the great cycles of energy on earth, are far harder to deal with, as we know by now to our consternation, than just the diffusion of invented artifacts and activity routines. Such management has so far notoriously failed even to eliminate all natural catastrophes brought on directly by human mistakes.

The species can boast better luck in overcoming deficiencies and disparities in natural habitat endowment by technical means, again of course through diffusion of innovations, not only in techniques as such but also in objects and systems of management, including economies, themselves diffusion phenomena. The vaunted distinction of using tools enables people to construct and manufacture things to offset the niggardliness of nature. Then what do we do? We move things to make things to serve us. Manufacture and trade furnish means of ecological compensation to enhance poor habitats, supplanting their meager endowments by transferring excess materials and energies from elsewhere. This export and import also constitutes diffusion.

In school, one used to recite humanity's primary needs: food, clothing, and shelter. Psychologists in particular have since extended the list to embrace a host of intangibles. Although such needs clearly vary in kind and intensity from culture to culture, and from one habitat to another, difussive interchange has been able to meet them for a fortunate minority of humankind. Still, the tragic inability (or disinclination?) to nourish and shelter and heal the rest of humanity that has to contend with niggardly habitats stands as a grave reproach and great challenge to existing institutions in the favored countries.

Human relationships with habitats exhibit almost as much particularity as do those established by animals and plants unless so buffered and altered artificially that their rigors become assuaged. The sharing of innovations through communication, that is, diffusion, contributes most to accomplishing that. It counts as but one among the natural processes that still and always determine the basic conditions of life for any human population.

Probably no habitat of human beings today exists in total isolation. Once in a while explorers discover an unfortunate "stone age people" in some remote locality, such as the Philippine or Amazonian forests, but even such folk will not have lived altogether immune to influence from the outside. Diffusion reaches even them, in much attenuated forms. Nevertheless, the dimensions of interdependence differ tremendously from one place to another, and effective everyday habitats do vary greatly in extent. Given the global reach of effects of advanced technology, all terrestrial habitats—even antarctic skies—now fall heavily under its influence, which hardly bears comparison with the puny effects of a Pygmy band's activities.

What constitutes the habitat of a Pygmy foraging in the deep Ituri Forest of Zaïre? Overwhelmingly, the embattled rain forest, along with a few marginal villages of farming folk who carry on sporadic trade with the Pygmies. Contrast that situation with a modern North American one, in which the environs of the home itself deliver at most a few excessively costly vegetables from the garden to the family table, and the yard a bathroom for the dog. Everything shaping and defining the life style comes from somewhere outside, far beyond the local habitat proper. In standard geographical terms, it might be said that this latter sort of habitat exemplifies the primacy of situational factors over natural site conditions. Most habitats occupied and utilized by human beings around the world fall somewhere between that of the Pygmy and that of Americans and Canadians, their qualities considerably colored by both site and situation.

"Situation" refers to placement in a larger areal context embodying communication linkages. Obviously those connections may enable people to live in much the same fashion across a very wide area, supplied by trade with material means of survival and participating in a dialog with distant interlocutors. A "site," on the other hand, connotes an immediate complex of localized features from which a population may draw for its sustenance. The relevance of one or the other concept to livelihood and survival varies vastly, as just illustrated above. But the circumstances of life in any community still depend on some sort of site factors, whatever their ecological character. And everyone lives in a localized habitat, if not a lonely one.

When a society has developed a highly "situational" ecological strategy, its members no longer depend on the desert, forest, or sea directly for their livelihood and security, but rather on gainful employment and commerce. Still they may have to prowl the aisles of supermarkets in search of their provender, to forage almost as the Pygmies do in their marches around the deep forest. Human beings in any habitat must always organize the food quest and the techniques supporting it in a similar fashion, although compelled to observe the requisite ceremonials that give them access to nurturing spaces.

Professor Heini Hediger, the great Swiss zookeeper, pioneered investigation of the ways of animals within their habitats, despite the fact that he studied the animals in zoos. He succeeded in tracing their daily movements and identifying various stations along their itineraries dedicated to resting, refuge, hunting and feeding, playing, courtship, hoarding supplies, and other well-marked activities. The same can be done with the movements of Pygmies. And yes, it has also been done with the movements of commuters, shoppers, and harried mothers in Sweden or America. Every habitat, then, could be similarly mapped.

A habitat thus comprises not only site conditions and situation as such but also its own spatial structure, which its inhabitants trace out in conducting their habitual itineraries. Consultation of its diagram reveals the resources and facilities exploited as well. The dynamics of behavior accounting for the habitat diagram would of course require explication, but the structure and its components lie open to view. The observer may see them in landscapes.

The modifications of habitat, and thus of environment, that are practiced by human communities to varied degrees depend for their effectiveness on invention and diffusion promoted by Geltung, for one thing, and further on systematic control and management. The communicative basis of adaptation is clear, and the distinctive character of human communication colors it strongly. The Geltung factor is never far to seek.

Both technological invention and managerial initiative yield personal Geltung and all the rewards stemming from it. Only the latter, entrepreneurial power, however, can possibly wreak harm. The most deadly poison, concocted in the laboratory but never adopted in commerce and then later spilled in some accident, produces no harm; secret weapons never put in the hands of the troops are not commonly lethal to whole

populations. Every technical intervention in nature, baneful or beneficial, occurs at someone's specific initiative and is carried out through
organized social enterprise. Any institution that can capture sufficient
control of communication in order to direct the concerted technical efforts of numbers of people possesses an opportunity to change the world
in some way, and thereby also the potentiality for doing injury to nature
or human beings or both. Peril inheres in all power.

No malevolence or negligence need figure in the actual labor resulting in damage. Quite on the contrary, environmental and societal impairment probably mostly ensue as the fruits of loyal, honest effort,
wrongly directed. Immersed in their given tasks and doing as well as they
can at them, pursuing only recognition and proportionate rewards, numerous completely ordinary, decent people, in harmonious collaboration, can all too often make unforeseen and costly mistakes. Eager for
Geltung justly acquired, working together within their allotted spatial
and temporal venues, obeying the rules, such companies of people are
the major culprits in the degradation of habitats, and sometimes the ruin
of regions. Given the tools, good will and good work can also accomplish bad things. The governing initiative held by the powerful, not the
fault of the underlings, determines the effects obtained.

The institution of property allocates to enterprises spheres of intervention into nature without consideration of ecology. By and large it
fixes no limits on the times or intensities of use and exploitation. The
spatial sectors affected undergo whatever transformations obey the dictates transmitted through the network holding jurisdiction. The work
that proceeds corresponds to specific objectives of economic gain and
individual self-promotion, within the time span prescribed by financial
and market considerations, not by natural rhythms or other ostensibly
extraneous factors. The spatiotemporal framework and even the technical program originate elsewhere, then come fully to bear on the site of
activity.

What outsiders see as irrational, flagrant abuse of the habitat frequently obeys a plausible rationality, the one of economic survival of the
individual or firm. Although heavily supervised, the volume of fishing in
British Columbia more closely reflects the number of licensed commercial boats and clamoring, big-spending sport enthusiasts than the dwin-
dling numbers of halibut, salmon, and herring. Logging crews always
threatened with layoffs readily obey the orders to clearcut the hillsides,
leaving a desolate scene behind, even if they do not hate trees as some
people unfairly claim. Prairie farmers desperately mine the soil just to

contend with their debts, unable to indulge in sustainable management. Pulp paper mills along the shore, struggling hard to stay in business, pump pollutants into the air that nobody owns and toxic metals into free waters. From their own standpoints, driven by the market, the offenders can argue that they have to act as they do.

Temporal pressures encourage a hasty harvesting of natural resources. Entrepreneurs have expensive loans to retire, workers to pay, commitments to meet to their buyers, all the sooner the better. Such financial factors likewise discourage any avoidable expenditure on measures reducing waste and pollution. Except for a small minority, the apathetic public seldom protests. Hungry for taxes, as well as susceptible to influence from politically powerful interests, government agencies and officials often prove reluctant to regulate too severely. Every institution's own perceived interests understandably come first. Blame not blindness but the balance sheet!

To be sure, an enterprise will often attempt to advance its interests through personal favors, lobbying, publicity, and other propitious communicative means, addressing either the general public or privileged decision makers and regulators. The potential of organized, well-financed corporations as advocates for what they want is awesome. Unlike the public and even a government, they stand to see what they spend on presents, pretexts, and propaganda reflected directly in profits. Their information networks are not neutral, their connections not uninfluential. The diffuse interests and scattered, meager resources of environmental critics can frequently not match theirs. The future sometimes is the loser.

Political correctives for environmental excess suffer from a limitation of their own. Irrespective of their occasional incorruptibility and dedication, the best of rulers and legislators cannot fail to put political survival first. Whoever lets go of an office relinquishes one opportunity for doing much good. Elected officials and even their civil service underlings have to hold onto their jobs to accomplish anything, and that requires discretion and restraint that may frustrate any hope for fearless crusades. Power has first to take care of itself. Even voluntary environmental defense organizations can fall prey to this principle of politics.

But does humanity have the power also to take the right steps in time to take care of itself? Will it ever know what to do? Is it ready and willing to take the right measures, no matter how costly? The last chapter offers a hope and a guess.

FOURTEEN

Conclusions ●

The argument that this book advances ought to warrant some final remarks concerning the implications of what has been said for the future conduct of human affairs. The sort of geographical and humanistic reasoning used, acknowledging but remaining independent of any given political commitment or connection, appears in the main, first of all, to substantiate the soundness and effectiveness of many attitudes and measures already widely advocated in reaction to prevalent misapprehensiveness. If any program of action for humanity is here suggested, it will not depart by too much from some of those currently publicized and here and there put into practice.

Although by no means indicting technology in general as the major culprit in causing our various crises, I should arraign those human technologies and simple behaviors specific to communication at every level as chiefly responsible. Communicative conduct, the Geltung it dispenses or denies, and the spatial expressions of their effects can, I believe, be held accountable for many or most of the present problems we face. I believe that any sure betterment of the human prospect would require a very much improved understanding of how and especially why we communicate and how we distribute thereby the influence, enterprise, and power that I have depicted as guiding collective action. No science exists as yet, to my knowledge, possessing the means of addressing these problems as well as is warranted. Humanity had better learn to respond more conscientiously to the ancient injunction, "*Gnothi seauton*"—know thyself.

The reflective reader will perhaps have arrived at some of the same conclusions that I do. So too, surely, have many other people without having had to attend to the tortuous arguments I have presented, but the latter at least provide what I hope is a novel and independent outlook on recognized problems that they also ponder, tending perhaps to reinforce their own resolution and bolster their hope.

In the meantime, in briefest summation, the argument herein advanced appears to prescribe the following rudimentary formulae for ideal restorative action. They differ but little from proposals already well diffused and commanding some Geltung of their own. Not much of a liberal, a Christian, or even a humanist myself, I do not propose them out of allegiance to any present political agenda, but entirely on the basis of the reasoning laid out in this essay. I simply think they make sense.

Since hierarchical order itself underlies so many of the problems I have identified, however, I cannot rightly appeal to large organizations, to governments and great corporations as such, to heed the following list of prescriptions. I can only address individuals, living participants in the dyadic communicative episodes that in the end shape our fate.

1. Respect the importance of place. Link policy and practice much more closely to the nature and needs of particular, localized situations. Beware absentee control.

2. Respect the importance of persons. Acknowledge everyone's human right to a place and a voice. Provide a livable place on earth and in some society for every human being. Salvation for humanity has always depended on sharing. Unemployment, homelessness, oppression, and penury penalize society itself in the final analysis. They still the free voices of individuals who might contribute something of worth to the endless dialog the species requires. Let everyone fully into humanity.

3. Respond compassionately to the inborn craving for Geltung in every individual by according to all, whatever their place, a sincere and humane respect and recognition. Abolish discrimination according to gender and age, race and culture, or disability. Acknowledge our common humanity—or, if you wish, take the command to "love thy neighbor" to heart.

4. Expose and deconstruct vanities. Laugh at our foolish pretensions! For those warped results of Geltung concern, seek to substitute mutual understanding and respect. Moderate the stresses of competition through institutional improvements and, where appropriate, ceremonial, as some societies appear to have learned long ago how to do. Let humane communication heal the anomie and inner insecurity that prompt vain dis-

play. Work to dethrone wealth and power as idols. Through patient, fair, and persuasive community initiative, disabuse publics, particularly youth, of the meretricious and seductive falsehoods some of the media diffuse. Make fame depend on genuine social responsibility.

5. Challenge spatial monopolies of power. Air out the smoke-filled rooms and let people in. Tear down the walls, open the doors. Let politics belong to everyone, for all are equally deserving to act as "political animals." Get rid of secrecy.

6. Oppose war. The diffusion of lethal armaments has sometime to stop if the species is to survive intact; this problem is open to straightforward solution, although it is difficult. In addition, reallocation and fragmentation of spatial jurisdiction in many parts of the world would improve communicative structures and render them more congenial to resident cultural traditions. This could markedly reduce intergroup tensions at several areal levels. A further potential means of defusing hostilities and preventing aggressions might lie in defanging the fierce exponents of force represented by many national communications media. Never cease striving for peace.

7. Help to empower all persons to achieve and advance as far as possible through better diffusion of knowledge and skills. Face up to the present faults in educational systems and all other institutions that influence individual careers. Anchor them more securely into existing local spatial arrangements, cultural traditions, and communicative practices. Re-create institutions.

8. Give heed to the indivisible global environment and treat it with prudent respect, wherever within it actions take place. An individual habitat affords no safe hiding place from grand natural cycles. Remember the total environment always.

9. Work to modulate population processes. At present, the attrition by disease or even the genocidal extermination of some communities constitutes an even more pressing problem than, elsewhere, numerical growth in densities. Some of the points just listed pertain to this very issue. Similarly, the spread and control of deadly diseases can be subsumed mostly under diffusion phenomena and dealt with in those terms.

But although not treated in this book, the matter of apparently runaway population growth deserves a minimal comment as well. The surging increase of regional human populations, regarded biologically and historically, partakes of the character of other essentially spontaneous natural processes. Not only human beings but also their habitats with all the other content, including equally proliferating and sometimes also rapidly mutating pathogens, are involved. The problem needs to be addressed in those terms. As other threatening natural processes sometimes do, the prudent response to it apparently will call in time, as already foreshadowed, for massive emergency spatial rearrangements and material redistributions. Diffusion of certain relevant technologies will play a role, too, but this will in all likelihood have to be followed eventually by deep-going reallocations of personal initiative within families and communities, which implies that individual Geltung may amount to the ultimate issue involved.

Although these recommendations coincide so closely with those issuing from diverse other quarters of late, they also follow logically and systematically from the conception of humane geography herein laid out. They stem from the conviction that a confident continuation of the immemorial trend of human development depicted in this book, toward ever more effective communication, should prove most apt as a means of safeguarding the species. Emphatically, though, the present correct and laudable efforts to address the world's greatest problems fall far short of the need and must be vastly increased and diffused in order to ensure eventual stabilization and security.

It may be that somehow, somewhere within the ambitiously novel perspective on the world of humanity opened in these pages, something may suggest yet more improved communicative means of attaining a safer tomorrow for human genes and the Geltung-rich cultures they shape.

A listing of all the books and articles either relevant to topics treated in this essay or consulted during its long gestation would require at least another volume. I should be glad to correspond with anyone wishing to know about relevant sources and inspirations. Therefore the items below include only those needed to clarify some of the issues raised.

Ardrey, Robert. 1966. *The territorial imperative: A personal inquiry into the animal origins of property and nations*. Boston: Atheneum.

Austin, John L. 1962. *How to do things with words*. William James Lectures, 1955. Cambridge: Harvard University Press.

Baudrillard, Jean. 1968. *Le système des objets*. Paris: Gallimard.

————. 1972. *Pour une critique de l'économie politique du signe*. Paris: Gallimard.

Bellugi, Ursula, A. Birle, T. Jernigan, D. Trauner, and S. Doherty. 1991. "Neuropsychological, neurological, and neuroanatomical profile of Williams Syndrome." *American Journal of Medical Genetics, Supplement* 6: 115–125.

Bellugi, Ursula, A. Birle, H. Neville, S. Doherty, and T. Jernigan. 1992. "Language, cognition, and brain organization in a neurodevelopmental disorder." In *Developmental behavioral neuroscience*, ed. M. Gunnar and C. Nelson. The Minnesota Symposia on Child Psychology. Hillsdale, N.J.: Erlbaum.

Blaut, James M. 1993. *The colonizer's model of the world: Geographical diffusionism and eurocentric history*. New York and London: Guilford.

Bourdieu, Pierre. 1979. *La distinction: Critique sociale du jugement.* Paris: Éditions de Minuit.

Crosby, Alfred W. 1987. *Ecological imperialism: The biological expansion of Europe, 900–1900.* Cambridge: Cambridge University Press.

Douglas, Mary, and Baron Isherwood. 1979. *The world of goods: Towards an anthropology of consumption.* London: Allen Lane.

Glacken, Clarence W. 1967. *Traces on the Rhodian shore: Nature and culture in Western thought from ancient times to the end of the eighteenth century.* Berkeley and Los Angeles: University of California Press.

Goffman, Erving. 1959. *The presentation of the self in everyday life.* Garden City, N.Y.: Doubleday Anchor.

———. 1967. *Interaction ritual: Essays on face to face behavior.* New York: Anchor Books.

———. 1970. *Strategic interaction.* Oxford: Blackwell.

———. 1971. *Relations in public: Microstudies of the public order.* New York: Harper Basic Books.

Gumilev, Leo. 1990. *Ethnogenesis and the biosphere.* Moscow: Progress Publishers.

Hägerstrand, Torsten. 1967. *Innovation diffusion as a spatial process.* Postscript and translation by Alan Pred. Chicago: University of Chicago Press.

Hall, Edward T. 1956. *The silent language.* Garden City, N.Y.: Doubleday.

———. 1966. *The hidden dimension.* Garden City, N.Y.: Doubleday.

———. 1976. *Beyond culture.* Garden City, N.Y.: Doubleday.

Hanks, William F. 1990. *Referential practice: Language and lived space among the Maya.* Chicago: University of Chicago Press.

Mauss, Marcel. 1954 (original 1925). *The gift.* London: L. Cohen & West.

Needham, Joseph H. 1985. *The great titration: Science and society in East and West.* Ann Arbor: University of Michigan Press.

Reynolds, Peter C. 1981. *On the evolution of human behavior: The argument from animals to man.* Berkeley and Los Angeles: University of California Press.

Richardson, Miles. 1984. *Place, experience, and symbol.* Geoscience and Man, no. 24. Baton Rouge: Lousiana State University Press.

Sack, Robert D. 1980. *Conceptions of space in social thought: A geographic perspective.* Minneapolis: University of Minnesota Press.

———. 1986. *Human territoriality: Its history and theory.* Cambridge: Cambridge University Press.

Sahlins, Marshall. 1976. *Culture and practical reason.* Chicago: University of Chicago Press.

Schwab, Martin. 1980. *Redehandeln: Eine institutionalle Sprechakttheorie.* Königstein / TS: Anton Hain Meisenheim.

Searle, John R. 1969. *Speech acts: An essay in the philosophy of language.* Cambridge: Cambridge University Press.

Smil, Vaclav. 1991. *General energetics: Energy in the biosphere and civilization.* New York: Wiley.

Smith, W. John. 1977. *The behavior of communicating: An ethnological approach.* Cambridge: Harvard University Press.

Sommer, Robert. 1969. *Personal space: The behavioral basis of design.* Englewood Cliffs, N.J.: Prentice Hall.

Tuan, Yi Fu. 1977. *Space and place: The perspective of experience.* Minneapolis: University of Minnesota Press.

Van Gennep, Arnold. 1909. *Les rites de passage.* Paris: Nourry.

Veblen, Thorstein. 1918 (original 1899). *The theory of the leisure class: An economic study of institutions.* New York: B. W. Huebsch.

Wagner, Philip L. 1960. *The human use of the earth.* Glencoe, Ill.: Free Press.

―――. 1972. *Environments and peoples.* Englewood Cliffs, N.J.: Prentice Hall.

―――. 1981. "Sport: Culture and geography." In *Space and time in geography: Essays dedicated to Torsten Hägerstrand,* pp. 85–108. Lund Studies in Geography, series B. Human Geography, no. 48. Lund, Sweden: Royal University of Lund, Department of Geography / CWK Gleerup.

―――. 1992. "Easy Zs (in homage to Wilbur Zelinsky)." *Names* 40 : 4.

Wheatley, Paul. 1971. *The pivot of the four quarters: A preliminary inquiry into the origins and character of the ancient Chinese city.* Reprint, Chicago: Aldine, 1977.

INDEX

●

A

Action: always muscular, 6; communication as only, 36, 115; Geltung effects of, 57; institutions as, 86, 89, 95–96; position and, 10; responses to, in communication, 13; venues for, 57–58; verbs and, 35

Adaptation, bodily structure in, 8; Geltung promotes, 12; human self in, 14

Addiction, Geltung and, 77

Age, Geltung effect of, 53–55

Agency, human, in nature, 2, 5, 36, 139; mechanical character of, 7–8; unintentional harm produced by, 136, 140, 143

Animals: display among, 12, 28–29, 32, 35, 109; and territoriality, 8–10

Apparel: Geltung affected by, 38, 52–53, 66

Appearance: cultivation of, 13; Geltung concerns only, 12–13, 20, 46; personal, effects of, on Geltung, 49–50, 52

Attention: communication and, 7, 48

Autonomy, spatial aspects of, 80–81, 82, 84

B

Behavior: communicative, genetic influences on, 11; communicative, source of major current problems,

145; experimental tendency, 19; exploratory tendency, 19; expressive tendency, 24; fight or flee, 19, 82; innate human Geltung seeking program, 2; selection of, 11

Bias, private, in utterance, 17–18

Body: appearance and Geltung, 51–52; human, active in display, 7; physical limitations of, 6, 8, 9

Boundaries: communication and, 6; rites of passage and transgression of, 83–87, 129

Buffering, ecological, 8

C

Castle, metaphor of, 87–89, 112

Celebrity and popularity: appeal of, 15; hazards of, 21, 47, 50–51

Ceremonial: culture embodied in, 62; ethnographic examples of, 26–28; imitative learning in, 84; income and, 44; labor as, 44; potlatch, 26–27; rites of passage, 61–62; social integration promoted by, 27; spatial sharing and, 83; venue, importance of, 86; warfare as, 62–63

Channels, communication, 25, 108–109, 115–116

Circuits, 29–30, 39, 40